Dill

Hope you will enjoy
this collection.

Fondest Love
Muz & Tood
13 April 2003

Suffolk Poems & Verse

Suffolk Poems & Verse

Contrasting Images of a Beloved County

ISBN 0 948134 56 9

a
Castell
publication

Castell Publishing Mendlesham Suffolk IP14 5RY

Contents

Suffolk Poems & Verse

A RURAL VIEW OF SUFFOLK - from New Suffolk Garland.

“Health smiles around thy richly wooded dales,
Luxuriant uplands, and refreshing vales;
Thy fields are like a fairy garden, wide,
Where art and nature are so close allied,
Their happy union has subdued the wild:
Their home is here, and beauty is their child!”
Fair district! Where I drew my Natal breath,
Awoke to life, and hope to sleep in death -
Where I have seen, and loved to see green nooks,
Have heard, and joyed to hear, thy murmuring brooks -
Where I beheld, and gladdened to behold,
Lime, elm, ash, beech, and towering oaks of old -
Where I have felt sink in my heart the beams
Of the bright sun, that glowed on hills and streams;
Fain would I hope, in honour of my theme,
This dream of loveliness no fictious dream!”

A DAY AT THE RACES - The origins of this little ditty are unknown but come from the early 19th century when the renowned Ipswich Races drew crowds from all over the country :

“With ruffles round my wrist, my boys,
And a long cane in my hand.
There was none that could with me compare
For a grand squire in the land.

Dashing along in a coach and four,
To Ipswich races straightway;
‘Twas there I lost ten thousand pounds
All in the course of a day.

And when returning home again,
My funds they grew so small,
I became a broken gentleman,
And forced to leave Hintlesham Hall.”

LEISTON ABBEY BY MOONLIGHT. - *The abbey, now in ruins, dates from 1383 when it replaced one destroyed by fire.*

"Imposing must have been the sight
Ere desolation found thee,
When morning breaking o'er thee bright,
With new-born glory crown'd thee:
When rising from thy neighbouring deep,
The eye of day survey'd thee;
Aroused thine inmates from their sleep,
And in his beams array'd thee.

. . . But yet more beautiful by far
Thy silent ruin sleeping
In the clear midnight, with that star
Through yonder archway peeping.
More beautiful that ivy fringe
That crests thy turrets hoary,
Touch'd by the moonbeams with a tinge
As of departed glory.
More spirit-stirring is the sound
Of night-winds softly sighing
Thy roofless walls and arches round,
And then in silence dying."

THE VALLEY OF FERN - *A little valley to be discovered behind Leeks Hill in Melton near Woodbridge :*

"There is a lone valley, few charms can it number,
  Compared with the lovely glens north of the Tweed;
No mountains enclose it where morning mists slumber,
  And it never has echoed the shepherd's soft reed.
No streamlet of crystal, its rocky banks laving,
  Flows through it, delighting the ear and the eye;
On its sides no proud forests, their foliage waving,
  Meet the gales of the autumn or summer winds sigh;
Yet by me it is prized, and full dearly I love it,
  And aft my steps thither, I pensively turn;
It has silence within, heaven's proud arch above it,
  And my fancy has named it the Valley of Fern."

A HORKEY SONG - *This is a song sung at the Aldringham harvest horkey in the late 19th century. Depending upon the mood of the time the verses were sometimes coarse and vulgar, sad and sentimental, or cheerful and jolly. Here are verses of the latter :*

"I wish I had a pint of beer
And sugare half a pound,
A bottle of gin to put wherein
And a spood to stir it round.

O Lord how sinners do increase -
They increase more and more.
Last night they stole the kitchen sink;
Tonight they'll have the door.

I wish I had ten thousand pales.
I'd pale my garden round
To keep those pigs with their long snouts
From rooting up my ground.

I wish I had ten thousand bricks.
I'd build my chimney higher
To keep those cats with their long tails
From blowing out my fire."

BY THE DEBEN - *By E. L. Fowler. The river Deben flows through central Suffolk from Debenham to the coast at Felixstowe Ferry :*

"Din red, the sun sinks in the westering sky,
  Through rose and gold of swiftly fading cloud,
Seeking darkness and its gift of peace;

Over the tawny ploughland, patient, strong,
  There drifts, intangible, the pearled river haze,
Grey-pink where sunset light shines through;

While, outstretched wings aslant, the seagulls flash
  And dive, a sudden flight of whirling snow,
A sudden wake of eddying spume,

  Behind the green and humpy plough, which moves,
Serenely straight, towards the wide silver line
  Of Suffolk tidal-river, misted, calm,
Still redolent of the open sea."

MURDER OF MARIA MARTEN - Maria Marten's murder by William Corder in the Red Barn at Polstead on 18th May 1824, has endured as one of the most famous crimes of 19th century England, spawning books, plays, films and verse. Here an old ballad gives Corder's side of the story :

"Come all you thoughtless young men, a warning take by me,
And think of my unhappy fate, to be hanged upon a tree;
My name is William Corder, to you I do declare,
I courted Maria Marten, most beautiful and fair.
I promised I would marry her upon a certain day,
Instead of that I was resolved to take her life away;
I went into her father's house the 18th day of May,
O come, my dear Maria, and let us fix the day.

If you'll meet me at the Red Barn, as sure as I have life,
I will take you to Ipswich town, and there make you my wife;
I straight went home and fetched my gun, my pickaxe and my spade,
I went into the Red Barn and there I dug her grave:
With heart so light she thought no harm to meet me she did go.
He (sic) murdered her all in the barn, and laid her body low;
The horrid deed that he had done, she lay bleeding in her gore,
Her bleeding and mangled body he threw on the Red Barn floor.

Now all things being silent she could not take no rest,
She appeared in her mother's house, who sucked her at her breast,
For many a long month or more her mind being sorely oppressed,
Neither night nor day she could not take no rest;
Her mother's night being so disturbed, she dream't three nights o'er,
her daugher she lay murdered upon the Red Barn floor;
She sent her father to the barn, where in the ground he thrust,
And there he found his daughter, mingled with the dust.

My trial is hard, I could not stand, most woeful was the sight,
When her jawbone was brought to prove, which pierc'd me to the heart;
His aged mother standing by, likewise his loving wife,
And with her grief her hair she tore, she scarcely could keep life.
Adieu, adieu, my loving friends, my glass is almost run,
On Monday next will be my last, when I am to be hung.
So you young men that do pass by, with pity look on me,
For murdering Maria Marten, I was hanged upon a tree."

SUFFOLK CHURCHES - Suffolk has a wealth of medieval churches which dot its landscape. Algernon Charles Swinbourne describes them thus:

"Far, and far between, in divers orders
Clear grey steeples cleave the low grey sky;
Fast and firm as time-unshaken warders,
Hearts made sure by faith, by hope made high.
These alone in all the wild sea-borders
Fear no blast of days and nights that die."

A SUFFOLK STREAM - Unnamed, this little stream represents the many which meander through the sheltered, undulating scenery of this tranquil county:

"It flows through flowery meads,
  Gladdening the herds that on its margin browse;
Its quiet bounty feeds
  The alders that o'er shade it with their boughs.

Gently it murmurs by
  The village churchyard, with a plaintive tone
Of dirge-like melody
For worth and beauty modest as its own.

More gaily now it sweeps
  By the small schoolhouse, in the sunshine bright,
And o'er the pebbles leaps,
Like happy hearts by holiday made bright."

JOHN LYDGATE - The west Suffolk village of Lidgate was the birthplace of John Lydgate. A monk of Bury Abbey, he became the 15th century equivalent of a Poet Laureate. His works included 'History, Siege and Destruction of Troy'; 'Life of St. Edmund'; 'Fall of Thebes' - written as a continuation of the 'Canterbury Tales' - and the 'Fall of Princes' in which he provides an insight into the history of a pretty Suffolk village, for he tells us he was -

"Born in a village which is called Lydgate
In olden time a famous castle town
In Danes time it was beaten down
Time when St. Edmund Martyr Maid and King
Was slain at Hoxne."

AN INVITATION TO THE WOODBRIDGE BAZAAR - Held on the 2nd & 3rd September 1841:

"Rouse, rouse from your slumbers, the birds are all singing,
Bright Phoebus has mounted his orient car:
All Woodbridge is stirring, the church bells are ringing,
And thousands are hastening to reach the Bazaar.

The stalls are all ranged, and the soft eye of beauty
Beams welcome on hundreds that flock from afar;
Here Pleasure in league with Religion and Duty,
Sheds the light of her lustre to gild the Bazaar.

Stand aside! clear the road! see, the crowd is advancing,
I hear the glad shout, and the cheering hurrah,
The steeds, as though proud of their riders, are prancing;
And coaches are racing to reach the Bazaar.

Ye sons of the Church! Oh, protect her from falling!
'Mid doubting and darkness your beacon and star:
Do your best to secure the high prize of your calling,
And rush to her aid through the Woodbridge Bazaar."

DEEP IN A SUFFOLK VALE - G. A. Squires

"Deep in a Suffolk vale there is a wide
  Slow rivulet within an ancient wood
Whose reaching boughs depend, on their green mood,
  A shy, subaqueous other world to hide -
Where, under many a waving weed, beside
  Long lily stems slow-swaying in its flood,
Low through the cool, dim, greenlit quietude
  Of forests all their own dark fishes glide.

Into its shadowy, unreflecting green
  A latter-day Narcissus might downpeer,
Gaze deep and deep, and, happier lost, serene
  Past memory of self, beyond all fear,
Dream life away; Echo above him lean -
  Still lean and call and sigh, and he not hear."

DUNWICH - It is not difficult to be inspired by Dunwich, an important East Anglian city in the Middle Ages and now a remote collection of cottages on the edge of the crumbing cliffs. Virtually all that was once here has been lost to the insatiable North Sea. The following selection of poems bring to life the eerie fascination this place inspires :

"Where the lone cliff uprears its rugged head,
Where frowns the ruin o'er the silent dead,
Where sweeps the billows on the lonely shore,
Where once the mighty lived, but live no more;
Where proudly frowned the convent's massy hall,
Where bards proclaimed, and warriors shared the feast,
Where ruled the barons, and where knelt the priest, -
There stood the city in its pride - 'tis gone!
Mocked at by crumbling pile, and mouldering stone,
And shapeless masses which the reckless power
of time hath hurled from ruined arch and tower!
O'er the lone spot, where shrines and pillared halls
once gorgeous shone, the clammy lizard crawls;
O'er the lone spot, where yawned the guarded fosse,
Creeps the wild bramble, and the spreading moss:
Oh! time hath bowed that lordly city's brow,
In which the mighty dwell - where dwell they now?"

And from Victor Allen:

"Here on this quiet hill beside the sea,
The soil is consecrated. Here the past
Keeps vigil by a fortalice of dreams
Where neither moat nor battlement remains
To give remembrance surer harbourage.

Tread softly - here the Roman trumpets rang,
The flambeaux of the Saxon Palace burned,
Here, Felix brought the Rood and raised his church,
And Viking sloops discharged their freight of death.

Tread gently - here the chiming towers proclaimed
Worship and faith. Within those vanished walls
Beauty kept open doors, and with her dwelt
Her comrade, Courage and her handmaid, Toil,
And busy hands and loving craftsmanship

Crowned Dunwich with that diadem of fame
Which barbed the envy of the ruthless sea.

Tread softly, traveller, in this meadowed shrine
Of ancient memories, England lies asleep."

. . . and this by Ethel Wynne Candwell :

" . . . For the waves care little for rank and station,
And the winds are whimpering round the dead,
Whose souls cry out at the desecration
That flung their bones on the ocean's bed.
Oh! waste and silence and desolation -
And a passing thought for the years long fled!"

and from Henry Dell :

"Thy pomp, thy pow'r O Dunwich, now's no more;
Lost is thy splendor, sunk in endless night,
Fair trade and commerce have forsook thy shore,
And all thy pristine glories vanish'd quite."

and finally:

"Oh Dunwich, jewel of Suffolk past'
Your wonders only now to see
On parchment and in stone inscribed
In some forgotten cemetery."

THE HARVEST SUPPER - Orlando Whistlecraft, born at Thwaite in 1810, became nationally known for his 'Weather Almanack' and 'Climate of England'. But he was also a poet and this short excerpt breathes life into what was a familiar annual event repeated all over East Anglia:

"A sumptuous banquet decks the table wide
And master, neighbours, reapers, skirt its side.
The supper done, the flowing horn goes round,
While healths are named and rustic strains abound."

THE FALL OF KING EDMUND - The East Anglian Saxon king Edmund was killed by the Danes at Hoxne (or so tradition asserts) on November 20th 870. Part of a ballad recounting his death includes :

". . . . He bleeds - the quivering arrow gnaws his breast;
He dies - and agonising sinks to rest.
Tradition tells the mournful tale,
And weeps at Sorrow's bloody wail; -
Fell superstition marks the place,
That sheltered Edmund's last distress;
And never, from that fatal day,
Have Hymen's votaries trod the way.
His spirit, by the pale moon's light,
Flits there, each sad revolving night."

GHOST TRAINS - The colourful history of the narrow gauge Southwold Railway, which ran from the main line at Halesworth to the resort of Southwold, became the butt of much affectionate humour. This verse by Michael Cave in contrast paints a more melancholy picture :

"The old familiar rails on more
Run by the marshes to the sea
But those I followed oft of yore
Across the land so dear to me
Still have their signal lights that shine
For ghost trains on the Southwold Line.

By Walberswick and Wenhaston
With Blythburgh lying 'twixt the two,
My phantom train still travels on,
'Mid haunting scenes I've wandered through,
And with it memories again
Come crowding through my restless brain.

The ferry by the ruined pier,
The windmill on the Common green,
The carrier's cart, with simple gear
Of oil lamps and a canvas screen
'Neath which I'd curl beneath the hay,
Homing from school for holiday.

The marshes and the Blackshore Inn,
The old salt works below the town,
The rope-walk, where I'd watch men spin
Their cordage, pacing up and down,
The Mayor, at Trinity Fair tide,
Mounting the roundabout's first ride.

All through the years these have been mine
As nightly I my dreams consign
To ghost trains on the Southwold Line."

EUSTON - Euston Park and woods, owned by the Duke of Grafton, provided peasant-poet Robert Bloomfield with many themes for his poetry which reached its peak with his classic work 'The Farmer's Boy' where he describes the charms of rural farming life. Yet despite his undoubted enthusiasm he was not physically cut out for manual work and by the age of fifteen had already left Suffolk (for a time) to work for his brother George, a shoemaker in London :

"Where noble Grafton spreads his rich domains,
Round Euston's water'd vale, and sloping plains,
Where woods and groves in solemn grandeur rise,
Where the kite brooding unmolested flies;
The woodcock and the painted pheasant race,
And skulking foxes, destin'd for the chase;
There Giles, untaught and unrepining, stray'd
Through every copse, and grove, and winding glade;
There his first thoughts to Nature's charms inclin'd,
That stamp devotion on th'inquiring mind.
A little farm his generous Master till'd,
Who with peculiar grace his station fill'd;
By deeds of hospitality endear'd,
Serv'd from affection, for his worth rever'd;
A happy Offspring blest his plenteous board,
His fields were fruitful, and his barns well stor'd,
And fourscore Ewes he fed, a sturdy team,
And lowing Kine that grazed beside the stream;
Unceasing industry he kept in view;
And never lack'd a job for Giles to do."

THE RICKINGHALLS - The high street divides Rickinghall near the Suffolk-Norfolk border into two villages, Inferior and Superior. Reginald T. Bellamy's poem provides a tongue-in-cheek analysis of the difference :

"At Rickinghall Superior
They hold their head up high;
An arrogant exterior,
A hard repellent eye,
Proclaim them as the best of men
Who keep their rightful station,
Bestowing on the rest of men
A frigid condemnation.
You may be hungry, weary or
Be desperately dry;
At Rickinghall Superior
They pass unheeded by.

But only step along the street
A matter of a few short feet
To Rickinghall Inferior
And humbler men you meet.
They never raise a query or
Demand the reason why,
But if they think
You need a drink,
A drink for you they buy.
And so, though maybe beerier,
They're better men, and cheerier,
At Rickinghall Inferior -
And that you can't deny!"

ENCLOSURE - The enclosing of many greens and commons in the second half of the 18th century, with scant regard to the consequences for those who grazed their stock there, led to a familiar rhyme of the period which went :

"They hang the man and flog the woman
Who steals the goose from off the Common;
But let the greater criminal loose
Who steals the Common from the goose."

SUFFOLK SKY - *by A. E. Tomlinson :*

"Remembering the sky that dies to make a town,
Hating the city's cave of constant night,
O hem of England's garment, never soil
The gentle adoration of your sky,
The soft clean sky that answers when you pray!

Cherish its song like some great covenant
Whose words reach to the mercy of the moon,
Cherish the golden peace that therein dwells,
Peace that weeps from all your trembling stars!
Jealously guard your lullaby of life,
Cherish your lanes from metamorphosis
To sudden streets! Pray that your furrows
May never with indignity of shops!
Don't let men make your silence din,
Your sun a dirge, day dark, night day,
Your land a mockery, God an ugly grin,
Sincerity a sham nailed to a rotting cross!

And, faithful Suffolk, sweet with sleepy space,
Cherish your horizontal isolation,
Cherish your sky, the index of your soul,
Your mighty marsh whose mud we dredge for dreams,
Your lazy landscape and recumbent charm,
The stirring fronds above familiar fields -
Preserve with these some scented amaranth
Of sighing moonlight from December seas,
That when we go to Suffolks yet unknown,
Memory, the orator for our hearts, will say,
'Farewell, farewell, sweet Suffolk, and farewell!' "

ST. EDMUNDSBURY ABBEY - *Only sparse ruins remain of what was one of England's greatest abbeys; burial place of King Edmund :*

"Seven hundred years have passed away since powerful and great,
St. Edmundsbury Abbey stood, in proud monastic state:
A bold, stupendous building then, a rich and holy pile,
None other abbey half so fam'd in Britain's sea-girt Isle."

THE GIPPING - *Suffolk is a county of delightful slow-flowing and meandering rivers. Here is a tribute to one of the smaller, the Gipping, from Elizabeth Cobbold of Margaret Catchpole fame :*

". . . What tho' thy neighbour Orwell boast
His variegated length of coast,
His busy trade and shipping;
Tell him that happiness may stray
Where pomp could never find the way,
And glide thro' vales with Gipping.

No envious sands thy course perplex,
No howling storms thy waters vex,
Their shores of verdure stripping;
Thy peaceful streams translucent glide,
While flow'rets bend on either side
To view themselves in Gipping . . "

THE RIVER ALDE - *by George Crabbe (1754-1832) :*

"With ceaseless motion comes and goes the tide
Flowing, it fills the channel vast and wide;
Then back to sea, with strong majestic sweep
It rolls, in ebb yet terrible and deep;
Here samphire-banks and salt-wort bound the flood
There stakes and sea-weeds withering on the mud;
And higher up, a ridge of all things base,
Which some strong tide has roll'd upon the place."

VALLEY OF THE BLYTH - *J. W. Gosling*

"In the Spring I've seen you, stretched beneath the eye,
  With the Reydon Marshes green against the sky.
In Summertime I've known you, when the tide's at rest,
  With Bulchamp Farm encircled by glory for the West.
In Winter weeks I've passed you, through storms of driving hail,
  The trees of old Hill Covert bent beneath the gale.
As from a child I've loved you, through the passing years;
  Dear Valley, now I leave you to hide my unshed tears."

THE ORFORD MONSTER - The 13th century chronicler Ralph de Coggeshall recounted the strange tale of a wild man captured in the nets of local fishermen at Orford in 1204. The Rev. F. R. Keightley. M.A. tells the tale in verse:

"At Orford on the Suffolk Coast
There stands a Castle old,
Built as a royal warden's post
When Norman Knights were bold.

Three lofty towers, still well preserved,
Surround the Central Keep;
A Chapel too can be observed;
Below - a dungeon deep.

No stranger tale was ever told
By monk or chronicler:
Than one this Castle can unfold,
As many do aver.

This story now I shall relate,
And tell as I am able,
Yet shall not vouch that I can state
What may be true or fable.

Two fishermen of Orford Town
Went out their fish to get,
And found some creature, black or brown,
Entangled in their net.

They hauled it in with all their strength.
And on the shore there lay -
A monster full six feet in length
That filled them with dismay.

With head and body of a man,
And cover'd thick with hair,
Save, like a tonsure, for a span
The skull itself was bare.

Instead of legs, it had a tail
With scales that on it hung,
And glistened like a coat of mail
Or bright Caparison.

The eyes were green, and large and round
  The nose was hooked and high,
The mouth gave utterance to a sound
  That seemed a human cry.

A crowd soon gathered, thick and fast,
  It number'd half the town,
While messengers were sent at last
  To bring the Warden down.

The Warden came, and in his train
  The Prior of Butley too,
Who was so learned that his fame
  Was known the Kingdom through.

The man-fish now that had been caught
  was on a waggon laid,
And to the Castle straight was brought
  And to a cell conveyed.

The Knights and Monks who dwelt around
  Assembled then to see
If any answer could be found
  To this strange mystery.

The Warden open'd the debate
  And said - "I only know
That sailors often tales relate
  Of maidens seen below,

If maidens, then mermen must be,
  And this seems one in truth,
Let's put him back into the sea,
  And show to him our ruth."

Up jumped the Prior: "Your pardon, Sir,
  But by this truth I stand,
That men and maidens only were
  Created for the land.

Why heed these sailors' idle talk?
  For this I shall go bail,
That men and maids were made to walk
  And not to flop a tail.

I know full well from Holy Writ
Without demur or cavil,
This monster's features seem to fit
A false god or a devil.

When I arrived upon the beach,
And saw him in the waggon,
I knew at once, as Scriptures teach,
It was the false god - Dragon.

That god was half a fish 'twas said,
And here are all the signs,
This Demon is the god that led
The heathen Philistines."

A Knight then said: "Sir Prior, I pray
To ask a question here.
Are these false gods alive today?
And can they thus appear?"

The Prior made answer: "You'll admit
That satan comes to view,
The thing is plain from Holy Writ,
Then why not Dragon too?

I think it wise this god should burn,
To ashes in the fire,
Lest he might in his anger turn
And work us something dire."

The Warden said: "Sir Prior, I grant
Your arguments are strong;
But yet another test I want
That we may do no wrong.

'Tis my desire that he should now
Into the Church be taken,
And you can prove by that, I trow,
That you are not mistaken.

If you should him a Merman find,
As I myself surmised,
You might, forsooth, convert his mind,
And have him straight baptised.

But if he be a demon foul,
  Then burn he must and will
For in the sea he still might prowl
  To work us something ill."

So to the Church he then was brought,
  And at the Altar there,
The Prior with book and candle sought
  To gain his soul by prayer.

The prior he prayed full long and well,
  Then showed to him the "Host,"
The monster gave a frightful yell,
  As tho' a soul were lost.

So back they forced him to return
  With tumult and with scorn;
And all agreed that he should burn
  Upon the morrow morn.

The morning came, the faggots were
  Beside the Moat heaped high;
And all the citizens were there
  To see the Demon die.

But when the Warden soldiers sent
  The monster forth to bear,
Upon a fruitless task they went
  The monster was not there.

The Prior did then dismiss the crowd,
  And said: "I know full well
The demon by my prayers was cow'd,
  And has gone back to hell."

But at the Castle Inn a wight,
  (Who did on liquor dote,)
Said - "I was out all yesternight,
  And slept beside the moat.

But when the early dawn arrived,
  A splash my slumbers rent,
It was the Monster who had dived
  From off the battlement.

He saw me, as I stood amazed,
  And made an angry sound,
And then his two huge arms he raised,
  And lashed his tail around.

I thought at first that I would try
  To stun him with a blow,
But then - he bigger was than I,
  And so I let him go.

I saw him last upon the sward,
  Go wriggling to the sea,
And if you don't believe my word
  A liar I must be."

But what is false, and what is true
  To indicate I fail,
So I must leave the task to you
  In this strange fishy tale."

IN IPSWICH DOCKS - *By James Pattinson*

"See this old ship that lies beside the quay,
  Her hatches open to marauding crews
Of stevedores and the whole galaxy
  Of agents and officials seeking dues.

See how the garbage clutters up her decks,
  Flows like a tide in every alleyway;
See how the cranes, bending their iron necks,
  Peck at her heart like vultures at their prey.

Yet she has queened it over wind and wave,
  Has thrust the waters from her with disdain,
Going her ways above the sailors' grave
  In fog, in blizzard and the monsoon rain.

And she has ridden stately on the foam
  Of the great oceans and the Middle Sea,
Where once Odysseus came sailing home
  To slay the suitors of Penelope."

Then she has bucked and trembled like a horse,
  Though now she lies so still, as if asleep,
As if she had forgotten how the force
  Of storms could make her creaking body leap.

Now clerks in offices add up the cost
  Of many cargoes, writing manifests;
Not thinking how this treasure may be tossed
  Like flotsam on the billows' flying crests.

And there she lies at rest, and cannot hear
  The salt sea thunder where the tempest rides,
Only the factory sirens hooting near,
  And the fouled water lapping at her sides."

EVENING ON A SUFFOLK MERE - *Alastair Davis*

"The twilight draws her dreaming veil across the sapphire sky
  And clothes the blurring mud-flats in a dim obscurity,
While all around the water croons her liquid lullaby
  Of things that were, of things that are, of things that are to be.

And down the swiftly flowing ebb, pour ancient memories,
  Stirring that lone world of fen to life from death-like sleep.
Portraying in her sentient soul her former energies
  When galleon, brigantine and yawl came thronging from the deep.

Until no longer wheels the sea-bird o'er a lonely marsh
  For, looming thro' the mists, the gabled roofs and walls appear
Of what was once old Orford town, and voices bluff and harsh
  Ring out once more with eerie sound across the glimmering marsh.

For time may ne'er dissolve, but only veil from us the past,
  Which changeless in eternity exists for evermore.
From out whose timeless depths sometimes a memory gleam is cast
  To give earth's former days rebirth upon Time's shifting shore.

And thus the vision I beheld one shadow-haunted night
  Upon a lonely Suffolk mere that borders on the sea,
When all that desolate still land was steeped in gleaming light
  And all the air was vibrant with God's moving mystery."

SUFFOLK HARVEST SONG - The ending of the summer harvest used to be celebrated with a Harvest Supper when the ale flowed freely and spirits ran high. Songs were sung, many a little bawdy. This by Alice Cochrane is a little more reflective :

"In the ten-acre field, where the sheaves all agleam
Are marshalled in golden array,
Hear the black-bearded waggoner call to his team,
'Tarn-ye, Darkie, wheesh-ho and away!'

By the bend of the stream with tall reeds overgrown
Let us seek out the idler's retreat,
See the velvety water-vole slip from her stone
At the sound of our trespassing feet.

No blue like the paleness of calm Suffolk skies,
No spell like the water's still charm,
No sound like the whirr of the pigeons that rise
From the clustered red roofs of the farm.

No scent like the breeze over Westleton Heath,
Making sport with the thistle-down showers;
It has gathered the salt of the tide in its breath
Where Dunwich bemoans her lost towers.

But the twilight creeps up and the shadows grow long,
'Tis good-bye to our harvest-time play;
The last load starts home with an echo of song,
'So tarn-ye, wheesh-ho and away!' "

THE ROAD TO THE SEA - J. W. Gosling

"The road to the sea is the road to go,
  By Sutton Heath when the west wind blow;
And the road to the coast is the road to take,
  When Blackheath woods in the sunshine wake.
The road to the shore is the road to ride,
  By Brightwell church in the eventide;
And the road to the waves is the best of all,
  For its home to me where the salt tides call."

THE TALE OF CRAZY MARY - *'Crazy Mary's Hole' is a hollow in the cliffs at Pakefield cut by a spring which once flowed across the beach near the tower of the old Pakefield lighthouse. These 19th century verses by John Barcroft tell the story of how it acquired the name :*

"In the cliffs that front the eastern gale,
Low cliffs of drift that chalder
And change to sand, there lies a swale
With willow and with alder.

The rains of winter scar its bed
And make it dank and brashy,
Its slopes by showers of summer fed,
Not seldom soft and lashy.

The wayfarer who would not fall
Had therefore best be wary
Crossing the hollow sailors call
The Hole of Crazy Mary.

Here long ago a maiden strayed
Beside her sailor lover
And looked into his eyes that made
A heaven of blue above her.

He kissed her lifted lips and she
Of kissing was not chary.
'The day that I come back from the sea
I here will meet my Mary.'

'Each morn,' she said, 'for thy dear sail
I here will watch the billow,
Nor here at dark-hour shall I fail
Before I press the pillow.'

She kissed his bended brow and he
Of kisses was not chary.
'Farewell! I'll soon come back from sea
And here will meet my Mary.'

They parted - he along the shore
Her gaze upon him bended
Till she could see his form no more
Then home she slowly wended.

The summer came. Beside its nest
Chirped linnet, crooned the culver.
Cold winter with bright berries dressed
The branches of the hulver.

Fair spring returned with many a flower
In croft and corn that croodles
From passing storm and fleeting shower
Bright buttercups and boodles.

Full many a barque from distant lands
Returned with sailors laden,
But never hastened o'er the sands
Her sailor to the maiden.

Some she had nursed as babies now
Had home with husbands steaded.
Grief more than time had touched her brow
And she was still unwedded.

Alas that those who laugh should die
And those who weep should linger!
That death the wretched passes by
Not healing with his finger!

She dwelt alone, the well-worn way.
At fleet-time she would follow
And watch the wave the live-long day
Crouch'd in the craggy hollow.

The ploughman as he passed the field
Would often stop and leave her
Some dainty that the dairies yield
Or best bit of his bever.

Women, by pity touch'd to tears,
Would strive to soothe her sorrow.
She only murmured in their ears:
'Perchance he'll come tomorrow.'

She had but one thought - love. But men,
With fancies light and lazy
As butterflies in flowery glen,
At last they called her crazy.

Then surely that day was her best
When pitying hands could take her
And lay her weary limbs to rest
In God's reposeful acre.

A mournful hollow, moaning sea,
We men whose fancies vary
Like shifting sands, what right have we
To speak of Crazy Mary?"

OLD SUFFOLK - Mollie Tatum's poem recalls the pretty Suffolk town of Lavenham, famed for its wealth of timber-framed houses. In its medieval hey-day it was the centre of the East Anglian cloth industry:

"But dread of the song of the thrush
  And you'll dream of Lavenham too,
With Flemings weaving their wool and yarn
  And tenterhooks by the old red barn,
And troughs of dyes of the richest shades
  Made from the flowers of old Suffolk glades
And culled by the hands of Flemish men.
  How fine to have known quaint Lavenham then!

With guildsmen riding up and down
  The cobbled ways of the little town
And planning the richest of old-time fairs
  For selling their wonderful, woven wares.
How fine to have seen the market then
  And heard the quaint bartering of Flemish men!

But dream of the song of the thrush
  And you'll dream of Lavenham too,
With burghers thronging the oak wool-hall,
  Giving gold for their church of St Peter and Paul.
Giving their love, and labour, and time,
  Planning and moulding its aisles sublime.
Oh to have lived in quaint Lavenham then,
  And see the church builded by those good men!

But dream of the song of the thrush
  And you'll dream of Lavenham now,
With its hill-top market bleak and bare
  And its guildhall with no men meeting there
And the inns where carousing is heard no more
  Of the Flemish men, as in days of yore.
But the minds of the slow, good, earnest men
  Are just as they were in Lavenham then.
The fairs and Flemings are no more,
  But it's Suffolk, really Suffolk,
Suffolk to the core."

A SOLDIER REMEMBERS - A soldier serving in the Suffolk regiment in Cyprus in 1958 remembers his homeland in this verse sent to the East Anglian Magazine :

"We still remember sparkling rivers and green fields
  The song of larks and sunset o'er the meads.
The smell of hay, a summer's eve,
  The village inn, the wheat cock sheave,

Nut brown ale, the rustic's tale.
  A five bar gate, the milkman's pail,
Fresh turned soil, the horse and cart,
  Pink cherry branch, the ploughman's art,

The baying hounds, a pigeon's nest,
  Ripe strawberry beds, fat chicken breast.
Roofs of thatch, a gentle cow,
  Green village pond, the blackthorn bough.

These we remember, though far away
  These we are proud of and always say:
These are England - our England.
  Home!"

THE CHRONICLE OF CASTEL FRAMLINGHAM - Mrs. E. B. Cowell :

"Oh Framlingham! grey Framlingham! thy lords have passed away,
  On them and over thee hath fallen the mantle of decay!
Thy ruin'd walls still crown the brow where ages they have tower'd
  But in thy holy chancel aisles lie many a noble Howard.
. . . . Within thy walls, in other days, held Saxon princes reign,
  And round thee reav'd the pirate lords, led by the robber Dane;
But when the Norman's iron hand ruled over hill and heath,
  Then grandeur reared thy stately roofs, and spendour dwelt beneath;
And green the park around thee spread, where glanced the graceful deer,
  And slowly glided the white swan along the glassy mere;
And through the shady avenues, the merry archer sprang,
  And to the joyous huntsman's horn, the woodland echoes rang;
And tapestry hung its storied folds around the banquet-room,
  And lamps within the chapel shrine, lit up the midnight's gloom,
And floated many a pennon fair, those battlements across,
  Where only waves the wild briar now, and spreads the yellow moss."

THE COMING OF SPRING - By Edward Fitzgerald:

“Then the clouds part,
  Swallows soaring between.
The Spring is alive
  And the meadows are green.

I jump up like made,
  Break the old pipe in twain
And away to the meadows,
  The meadows again.”

COVEHITHE - Agnes Strickland describes the deserted ruins of its once great church :

“On gray Covehithe mild eve has cast
  A soft and mellow ray,
But o’er its glories time has passed
  With dark destroying sway.

All roofless now, the stately pile
  And rent the arches tall;
Through which with bright departing smile
  The western sunbeams fall.

The ivy wreaths unheeded twine
  In wild profusion there,
And oft with summer’s flowers combine
  To crown the oriel fair.

The choir is hushed, and silent now
  The organ’s thrilling sigh,
Yet swelleth ever from many a bough
  The linnets’ lullaby.

The grass-grown aisles, all green and lone,
  No musing footsteps tread,
And even o’er the altar stone
  The mantling brambles spread.

Tradition’s voice forgets to tell
  Whose ashes sleep below,
And fancy here unchecked may swell
  And bid the story flow.”

KENTWELL - E. H. describing the passing of a summer's day from the mile-long avenue which leads to the Elizabethan Kentwell Hall in Long Melford, a remarkable Suffolk village dating from Roman times and containing two great Elizabethan manor houses and arguably the county's most imposing church set beside the lovely village green.

"Here in the light of cool declining day,
  Melford! beneath thy goodly limes I stray,
Whose lofty arms embracing high o'erhead,
  In one long arch of verdure o'er one spread.
Fair trees! tonight no bird your calm invades,
  No rustling breeze disturbs your peaceful shades;
Yon distant sound that breaks upon the scene,
  Come faintly wafted from the village green,
Where late I watched them, rosy, wild and gay
  A troop of sturdy youngsters at their play.
Intent the ball with dext'rous aim to throw,
  Or deal with ready bat the stinging blow.
Such sounds but serve to deepen nature's calm,
  And to her stillness add a threefold charm.

Where yonder church its stately pile uprears,
  Undimmed in splendour thro' the mists of years.
I stood and watched the light of evening fade
  Along these boughs, till, shade succeeding shade
Like lofty hills enwrapped in gloom they stood
  On the dark confines of some trackless wood,
Now sheltered 'neath their massy depths I view
  The last warm sunset rays that filter through,
And pleased from out the trembling leaves espy
  The first pale star that twinkles in the sky.
Low in the east, half lost in twilight haze,
  The distant hills of Essex meet the gaze;
There busy Halstead sleeps, serene and still
  On the green terrace of her Colne-washed hill,
And many a rustic farm and homestead lone
  Hides in those vales, unknowing and unknown.

Here on each side extends a grassy mead,
  Whereon a group of quiet oxen feed;
While darkly seen against the fading sky,
  Loom out in bold relief yon elm-trees high,
O'er whose broad heads aloft in rich array

Floats one bright cloud, all crimson, gold and grey
That, while I gaze, like some fair spirit blest,
Melts out of view adown the purple west.

At length the boughs divide, a flood of light!
And Kentwell's ancient hall appears in sight;
Towards its iron gates, across the glade,
In narrowing lines a level path is laid,
Along whose smooth expanse, of radiance small,
Surprised I mark the trembling moonlight fall.
Now, as my path reluctant I retrace,
Between the leaves fair luna shows her face,
Serenely bright, and woodland, hill and plain
Own the calm glory of her lustrous reign.

Still, Melford! may thy trees in beauty grow,
And o'er the glade their grateful shadow throw:
Still from yon sacred aisles, as now I hear,
May the soft pealing organ charm the ear,
And still as now, when rosy day hath fled,
Yon moon shine calm and cloudless overhead;
For, oft as thro' her sunny shire I roam,
Methinks fair Suffolk hath no fairer village home!"

BUNGAY NAVIGATION - A caustic response from the townspeople of Bungay to plans to extend the navigable section of the river Waveney to Diss in Norfolk; a dream which remained unfulfilled:

"You've heard of Old Bungay, - her fam'd Navigation, -
Her Waveney, the pride and delight of her Town; -
That brings to her Wharf the choice wares of the Nation;
And adds every year to her wealth and renown.
You've heard too of Diss, and her Duck-Pond or puddle;
Her Mere, fam'd for mud, and of reptiles the den; -
You've heard of Diss Beer, which we drink, - and not fuddle
Of her Ginger-bread Cakes and her Diss-honest Men!
And now you shall hear how these Diss-honest fellows,
Have a project to make us all wonder and stare;
'Tis to steal all the Trade from Old Bungay, - they tell us -
By joining Diss Pond to the Waveney and Yare."

TOLLY AND COBBOLD - A Tale of two Suffolk Brewery families by Arthur C. C. Hervey. Before their amalgamation, Tollemache and Cobbold were rivals for the lucrative Ipswich trade :

"In every street round Ipswich way
Two rivals you are sure to find;
Wherever Tolly takes his stand
Cobbold's not far behind.

Where Tolly sets Lord Raglan up
There Cobbold just across the walk
To keep an eye upon his moves
Stations the Duke of York.

And no good hunting can be done
And nothing but frustrations loom
When one camp holds the Fox and Hounds
T'other the Horse and Groom.

But near the County Hall - mark well
Incipient germ of brotherly love -
Tolly put forth the Olive leaf,
Cobbold supplied the Dove.

One notion to another leads
Till it becomes accomplished fact
These former deadly enemies
Join in a friendly pact.

But still we must take leave to doubt
Whether these now so friendly two
Are yet prepared to testify
Guinness is good for you!"

SLAUGHDEN, ORFORD & THE ALDE - by George Crabbe:

"There stands a vale beside the rolling sea;
  Hail, Slaughden, hail! my theme belongs to thee;
Thy boundless prospect charms the wand'ring eye,
  The rising waves that kiss the azure sky,
The white sail shining from some distant skiff,
  The level beach, the rough aspiring cliff,
The castle's mouldering wall, the silent wood,
  The silver face of Alde's meandering flood."

THE BATTLE OF SOLE BAY - *On May 28th 1672 a great sea battle was fought off Easton Ness between De Ruyter's Dutch fleet and the English and French fleets under the Duke of York. The French withdrew the flagship The Royal James was lost and the Earl of Sandwich killed. Despite the patriotic enthusiasm of the following onlooker, both sides claimed victory and it was historically pronounced a draw!* :

"One day as I was sitting still
Upon the side of Dunwich Hill,
And looking on the ocean,
By chance I saw De Ruyter's fleet
With Royal James's squadron meet;
In sooth it was a noble treat
To see that brave commotion."

Well might you hear their guns, I guess,
From Sizewell-gap to Easton-ness,
The show was rare and sightly;
They battered without let or stay,
Until the evening of that day:
'Twas then the Dutchmen ran away -
The Duke had beat them tightly."

PIN MILL - *by F. H. A. Engleheart. This enchanting and unspoilt little boating hamlet lies on the banks of the river Orwell a short distance down river from the busy port of Ipswich:*

"The honey light on the tree marbled hills
Across the estuary entrammels us.
We are held captive, not as is the fly,
Cased and embalmed in amber long ago,
But as a lover stands and gazes thus,
Caught in a quiet, caring but to know
His heaven is here; this light, this drench of sky,
heals us and stills.

But the eye wanders as the sunshafts lower.
Here is a wash of oyster-coloured ooze
Tongued with the turquoise thrusting of the flood,
The insinuating seas that, twisting wry
In a Suffolk tideway spill their strength and lose
The aspiring water welling in a sigh.
Here is the press of an insistent blood,
The pulse of power.

It vivifies; it fills. Here in the bay
The leaning masts, awakening, ride upright.
As jewels move upon a breathing breast
So gently sway the little coloured craft
On this resurgent bosom. Lifting light
They swing to the stream. Landward a voice has laughed
Out of the huddle of homes that proffer rest
  At the close of the day.

High water and the night . . . Shall we embark?
On some dream ship drop seaward with the tide -
To what adventurous storm that swings and stamps,
Or to what Eden isles beyond the charts?
Or shall we stay and take the valley-wide
And brimming nocturne to our wondering hearts,
The sinuous glimmering of reflected lamps
  And whispers in the dark?"

FISH QUAY - by A. E. Tomlinson. From the 14th century Lowestoft was a major East Coast fishing port. In the 19th century 300 fishing boats were employed in the herring industry. The trade has now all but vanished and the town, with its fine sandy beaches, has been revitalised as a popular seaside resort :

"I see sunlight running like cold slime
From netted mounds of fish on Lowestoft quay,
I see men whose trade is as old as time,
And like a great robbed grave, I see the sea;
I see the columned concrete of the dock,
And rubber marks in dust where men have trod,
Like shaken trees I see the quay masts rock,
I smell the wrathful silence of caught cod!
Packed like new gloves in ignominious ice
I see the sea's coiled flesh as white as lime,
I hear the hoarse tradesmen shouting out its price;
Where sun and fish-blood run like dredgered slime
I feel cold winds chase shadows down the quay,
And on the wind, the space smell of the sea."

A SUFFOLK COURTSHIP - *Taken from the East Anglian Magazine.*

"Lor', Mary, love me pray now dew.
To you I wull be kind and trew
And all the money I can arn
A-troshin' in my marster's barn
Each Sarridy night I wull give yew.
So love me, Mary, pray now dew.

Lor', John, I don't know what you mean.
Besides, if in this place I'm seen,
My missus she will rip and scowld
And say I am a hussy bold.
So go, John bor, less hev no wuds -
I'm busy with my whey and cuds.

Lor', pretty mawther, pray don't go.
It is somehow I like yew so
Yar missus she may rip and scowd
Lor', drat it, she ont allus 'owd.
Lor', Mary, wull yew go to the fair?
I'll axe me marster for his mare
And yew shall nicely ride, my dear -
Nit upon the mare's bare back,
Nit upon a hempen sack,
But a pillion I wull sartin find
And all things for to plaze your mind.

Lor', thank yer, John, I canna go.
My bonnet and gown are but so-so.
My gloves are so small they ont go on.
So I shall not see the fair, kind John.

Yes, that yew shall, for dew yew see
I've got guineas, one tew, tree.
Tew shall yew hev fer your own sel'
For more I like yew tidy well.
Lor', Mary, will yew be my wife?
Happy we'll live and hev no strife.
I'll work all day with joy and glee,
At night come home my wife to see.
In summer I will dig and louh
And you shall milk the brindle cow.

Our garden, tew, we wull keep drest
And we'll hev strawberries the wery best.
Our landlord when he come at autumn
Wull find how well that we can treat 'um.
His lordship we wull keep in tune
And he shall hev the silver spune.

Lor', John, I donna what to say.
I canna wery well say nay.
But ont that love of yars grow cowd?
Wull it continue when I'm owd?
Remember, John, I'm in my yuth.
I hope you spoke the words of truth,
For if you from your love depart
You'll break poor Mary's tender heart.

Lor', pretty mawther, if I larf
I wish my cow might never calf,
I wish the birds might steal my wheat
And so that I had none to eat.
If with a cliver I do cut
I wish it be my hand or fut,
If you should ever live to see
The slightest change of love in me.

Lor', John, you alter me now quite,
I fare somehow so quare tonight.
My missus she may rip and scowld -
I don't care for ought she's towld.
So one sweet kiss before we part.
From this time, John, you're my sweetheart."

SUFFOLK MIST - *Cloudesley Brereton :*

"Now steals the mist with its powder puff
And powders the gable's brick-red nose,
And round the chimney's slim neck throws
A daintily-puckered ruff;
And gowns the raggle-taggle trees
All battered and torn, and ill at ease,
With its linsey-woolsey stuff."

SUFFOLK - from 'A Suffolk Largess'. The Suffolk coast and along the river Orwell to Ipswich :

"While poets in bright fantasy delight,
Or for a theme to foreign fields take flight,
I choose thee, Suffolk! with thy piercing breeze,
Thy well-form'd team-horse, porkers, malt and cheese,
Whose virtues all thy native bard set forth,
Nor have they lost an atom of their worth;
But since his time have Suffolk men unfurl'd
Improvement's flag, and given to the world
Of agriculture instruments whose fame
have won for thee a never-dying name.

To thy bleak shore and health-bestowing air,
From distant parts right many now repair:
Lowestoft, once for nought but fishing gear
Renown'd, now owns its terraces and pier;
And Aldborough and ancient Southwold, each
Can boast attractions on its rugged beach;
And, farther south, full well do tourists know
Brave landguard Fort and pretty Felixstow,
Whence on to Ipswich flows the river's tide,
'Twixt lovely spots which smile on either side;
Here Woolverstone delights the passer's eye -
There Nacton's oak their branches wave on high.

Nacton! than thee flat Suffolk cannot boast
A sweeter village on her sandy coast.
Thy 'Hall', thy 'Park', both picturesque and grand,
Half hid by foliage on fair Orwell's strand;
Thy yellow whins and spreading chestnut-trees,
Which swell thy beauties and perfume the breeze;
Thy mossy church, the poorhouse on the mound;
Thy thick-grown covert, where at eve resound
Thy nightingale's soft warblings, and the crow
Of pheasant-cocks as to their roosts they go -
All tend to make thee, Nacton, what thou art,
Fit scene to charm the bard of nature's heart.

Nor, quiet Dunwich! must thou be forgot,
(By pleasure-folk, a much-frequented spot),
Once ranked chief 'mong cities of the East,
Now of our sea-side villages the least;

For all thy grandeur, which in days of yore
Was meet for monarchs, now is seen no more;
All by that mighty despot, Neptune, ta'en,
And buried in the sand of his domain.
And even yet, when from the rough north-west
The blustering wind disturbs the ocean's breast,
The seething waves their foam-crown'd heads uplift,
And batter down thy rotten yielding clift:
Still, charms e'en now are found thy shades among,
In praise of which well thy own poet sung.

Yes! Suffolk, much I prize thy fertile soil,
Land of true enterprise and honest toil!"

THE FARMER'S BOY - Two excerpts from Robert Bloomfield's classic work which covered the four seasons and ran to 1500 lines :

"Here midst the boldest triumphs of her worth,
Nature herself invites the reapers forth;
Dares the keen sickle from its twelvemonth's rest,
And gives the ardour which in every breast
From infancy to age alike appears,
When the first sheaf its plumy top uprears.
No rake take here what heaven to all bestowes -
Children of want, for you the bounty flows!
And every cottage from the plenteous store
Receives a burden nightly at its door.

Hark! where the sweeping scythe now rips along
Each sturdy Mower, emulous and strong,
Whose writhing form meridian heat defies,
Bends o'er his work, and every sinew tries;
Prostrates the waving treasure at his feet,
But spares the rising clover, short and sweet . . ."

and on his native village - HONINGTON IN SPRING

"Come to thy native groves and fruitful fields;
Thou know'st the fragrance that the wild-flow'r yields;
Inhale the breeze that bends the purple bud
And plays along the margin of the wood".

SUFFOLK HARVEST - *From 'The Enchanted Wood' by Sir Francis Newbolt :*

"The Suffolk skies are pale and bright
Its ocean airs are keen,
Dark and Jolly is hedgerow holly
With white stems in between.
A peasant woman homely dight
Gleans slowly in the pure twilight
Where harvesters have been."

A SUFFOLK MEADOW - *D. E. B., East Anglian Magazine :*

"Silver grey the willows fringe the reedy pool,
Leaning over waters, curdled, green and cool,
Where the sleepy cattle drink at close of day,
Winding through the meadows on their languorous way.

Idly now the plundering bee has boomed its way
Over fragrant hedgerows set with starry may;
Rifling flowery thickets where wild roses meet
Firstling drifts of snowy scented meadow-sweet.

Rust red the sorrel stains the dappling grass,
Tawny-headed thistles wave as breezes pass.
Tossing burdened branches of the wooded glades,
Whispering through a myriad sparkling emerald blades.

Mellow falls the sunlight, where the poplars sway,
Over distant homesteads, gracious in decay;
Falls on crumbling rafters, creviced lichened eaves;
Timbered gables thick with summer's latticed leaves.

Nature like a spendthrift, scatters largesse here,
Through the ever-changing seasons of the year.
And time himself would lose one hour from his great store,
Lingering in this shady quietness once more.

Here where men must labour, plant, and sow, and reap,
Peace broods eternal, from the fields of sleep.
Swiftly idle moments slip their leash, and pass
Down in the meadow, in the waving grass."

FAKENHAM MAGNA - *Poet Robert Bloomfield describing Fakenham Magna his Suffolk home by the Black Bourn river :*

"On thy calm joys with what delight I dream,
Thou dear green valley of my native stream!
Fancy o'er thee still waves th'enchanting wand,
And every nook of thine is fairy land."

And on the mansion said to have stood within the earthworks known as Burnthall Plantation :

" . . . but its day is o'er;
The moat remains, the dwelling is no more!
Its name denotes its melancholy fall,
For village children call the spot 'Burnt-Hall' "

BRECKLAND - *Thomson describes the area of North West Suffolk where the light sandy soil attracted the earliest settlers to the county :*

"And Suffolk! Thou has many a spot
Thus marked for immortality;
Which those who feel their worth, would not
Willingly, carelessly, let die;
Because the dead of days gone by
Have there done, suffer'd or enjoyed,
What lies in faithful memory
To snatch them from Oblivion's void.

And purple all the ground with vernal flowers
Bring the rathe primrose that forsaken dies,
The tufted toe-crow, and pale jessamine,
The white pink, and the pansy flecked with jet,
The glowing violet,
The musk-rose, and the well-arrired woodbine,
And every flower that sad embroidery wears.

. . . . Plains immense
Lie stretch'd below, interminable meads
And vast savannahs where the wandering eye,
Unfixt, is in a verdant ocean lost."

THE WAVENEY - *Jean Ingelow on the river which forms the Suffolk-Norfolk boundary :*

"Listen to me -
There is a little river, fed by rills
That winds among the hills,
And turns and suns itself unceasingly,
And wanders through the cornfields wooingly,
For it has nothing else to do, but play
Along its cheery way:
Not like great rivers that in locks are bound,
On whom hard men doth heavy burdens lay,
And fret their waters into foam and spray.
This river's life is one long holiday
All year round.

Listen and long -
It hears the bells of many churches chime,
It has a pleasant time:
The trees that bow to it their branches strong,
Hide many birds that make its spring one song;
And orchard boughs let fall their flowery wealth,
And float away by stealth,
And land in tiny coves a mile below,
Or round and round the stems of rushes veer
Like snowy foam, but truly none is here,
So calmly gurgle on the waters clear
with endless flow."

SUMMER EVENING IN GREAT BEALINGS CHURCHYARD - *Bernard Barton:*

"It is not only while we look upon
A lovely landscape that its beauties please;
In distant days when we afar are gone
From such, in fancy's idle reveries,
Or moods of mind which memory loves to seize,
It comes in living beauty, fresh as when
We first beheld it: valley, hill or trees
O'er shadowing unseen brooks; or outstretched fen,
With cattle sprinkled o'er exist, and charm again."

Partial to a drink and a game of cards, SQUIRE WILLIAM COE *was a familiar figure around 18th century West Row. He kept a diary and one strange entry for February 14th 1700 reads: 'Mr. Eldred of Bury cut off my girls' hair, viz : Judith, Anne and Elizabeth, to make me a wig, 1½ ounces bare weight', later led to a poem by Mortimer Collins printed in 'All the Year Round':*

"Where's Squire Coe of fair West Row,
  In the days of William and Mary?
The squire who with punch defied all care
  And made a wig of his daughters' hair?

Lo, where they sit, these maidens three,
  A sight for young beholders,
With viol or book upon shapely knee,
  Long locks over rose-white shoulders;

No trace of grief in their mien appears,
  And they look demurely merry,
Though they wait, alas! for the fatal shears
  That the barber brings from Bury;
No fairer Anglians ere drew breath
  Than Judith, Anne and Elizabeth.

Ah! what would say the Suffolk girl
  In these days of advanced opinion,
If asked to yield but one bright curl
  That veils her voluminous chignon?

What Suffolk Squire, though never a hair
  His sterile scalp can harbour,
To share his daughters' tresses dare
  Send for the Bury barber?
'Tis well Squire Coe in the mould lies low,
  For this is a world he scarce would know."

THOMAS GAINSBOROUGH - From the Suffolk Garland of 1788, a tribute to Thomas Gainsborough by an unknown author who laments his passing:

"Mourn, Painting, mourn, recline thy drooping head,
  And fling thy useless pallet (sic) on the ground!
Gainsborough is numbered with the silent dead,
  And plaintive sighs from hills and vales resound.

His genius lov'd his country's native views,
  Its tapered spires, green lawns, and sheltered farms:
He touch'd each scene with nature's genuine hues,
  And gave the English Landscape all its charms.

Who now shall paint mild evening's tranquil hours,
  The cattle slow returning from the plain,
The glow of sultry noon, the transient show'r,
  The dark brown furrows rich with golden grain?

Who shall describe the cool sequester'd spot,
  Where winding riv'lets through the willows glide;
Or paint the manners of the humble cot,
  Where meek content and poverty reside?"

THE VILLAGE - Some thoughts on the village of Yoxford (known as the 'Garden of Suffolk') by the poet James Bird (1788-1839) :

"Oh! in a spot so fair as this,
Which nature's heavenly hand
Has painted for her bower of bliss,
Her Eden of the land;
In this fair spot life's stream should glide,
One sweet, unchanged, unbroken tide.

Dear, peaceful village! though from thee
My thoughts are wont to roam
To distant scenes o'er earth and sea,
Thou only art my home;
In thee alone my treasure lies -
My all of joy beneath the skies!

Beside me sweeps the spreading glade;
Around me spring the flowers;
And far below, amid the shade
Of happy green wood bowers,
All bright beneath the spangled skies,
My loved and lovely village lies."

SONNET TO GREAT BLAKENHAM - *Miss S. Evance*

" . . . where riv'lets wind,
Thy cornfields, waving 'neath the rustling breeze,
And thy secluded copses - they are dear
To me; and when I go far, far away,
Full oft amid thy scenes will memory stray.
Ah! virtue, taste, refinement pure are here;
And these, when view'd by fond affection's eye,
Give thee an interest - which shall never die!"

EXILE FROM SUFFOLK - *By Reginald T. Bellamy* :

"Oh some day I must go again
To Cavendish and Clare;
And stand and watch the dimpling rain
Upon the river there;
And I must go in winter-time
Before my days are done,
Along a Suffolk road when rime
Is glinting in the sun.

And some time I must make my way
To where the quiet Stour
Runs slow beneath the drooping may;
And I must see the tower
Of Melford church gleam clear and bright
Above the shadowed woods
On fickle days of changing light,
When April flaunts her moods.

In hill-top farms the windows flame
With dawn and sunset glow,
And people there are much the same
As people years ago;
And whether harvest crowns the hill
Or fields lie wet and bare,
I know that beauty beckons still
From Cavendish and Clare."

THE EMPTY GRAVE - This poem of the great Saxon Ship Burial at Sutton Hoo won for its writer, F. H. A. Engleheart, the Crabbe Memorial Poetry Competition in 1956 :

"There was a stir at Blythburgh
  When there they brought the king
And laid him with his one loved son
Because the Mercian men had done
  A sore and fearful thing.

They came to slay but when they slew
King Anna and his heir
They loosed a thing no man could bind:
Kindling the foe to furious mind,
As a flame leaping on the wind
  It beat them to their lair.

Straight and still in the house of God
  father and offspring lay.
On the waxen faces guttering lights
  Flickered time away.

Then Aethelhere, as the new king cried:
  'Here shall our brother lie
In his faith, but we'll have a burial too
In the way our House was wont to do,
In the time-worn way at the kingly Hoo,
And none shall ask me why.'

At Kingston and at Rendlesham
  They combed the weapon hoard
In a great sea boat at the waiting quay
They built a shrine of chieftaincy;
The rune they wrote on the high roof-tree
  Was deeply scored.

A cloak and the clasp of golden snakes
They brought for the king's last home,
His harp, a nest of silver bowls,
  The spoons from Rome.

They took and mended the dragon shield,
  held from an older day,

And the graven helmet of beaten bronze
  With gold inlay.

The wrights and goldsmiths furbished new
  The one-time Swedish sword
With its tracery-gold and garnet hilt
  For the English lord;

With the scabbard to sheathe in stone-set hide
  The ripple-welded blade
And the whistling song of sundering
  It made.

These and more in the mid-ship shrine -
  With a purse - they laid with care,
And the whetstone badge of the Sharpening One
  Who was not there.

Bright was the gleam of the laden boat,
  The stones shone rich as blood
As thirty oarsmen manned their sweeps
  And the ship slid out of the heathland steeps,
Slowly out on the flood.

Under the sheer of Sutton Hill
  She nosed the shelving shore,
And, hauled up in her moorings, lay,
  As loath to leave the water's play,
The river's and the sea's low say,
  Their laughter and their lore;

The same wide sea that curled and swung
  With a strange weight of will,
The swingeing dragon hiss that drave
  In seethe and thunder of the wave,
In shout and song and saga brave -
  Way out behind the hill.

But ropes were bent and men in scores
  Wrestled her up the turf,
Hauled and hove till the tow was cast
  And she lay, her loftiest comber passed,
Overwhelmed in earth.

High they heaped that bier with turves,
  The burial wake near done.

Knight and thane trod their farewell
  Around it - and were gone.
Back to the earth, there, went again
  The glister and wealth men borrow . . .
A year was gone . . . and five . . . and ten;
  And all these things seemed cloudier then,
And the kin who had grieved for the taken men
  Forgot their sorrow."

A SUFFOLK VETERAN - *D. E. B., East Anglian Magazine* :

"Why come right in! Where hev yow bin tew bor?
Take off yar coat and fasten that there door.
Thass crewel co'd ter day. I'm wholly friz;
I sit in draughts and git the rheumatiz.
The doctor think me wittles don't agree,
But darn the man! I take n' heed o' he.
The duzzy fule he say, 'Now no more bare!'
He shout that twice, same's if I couldn't hare.
The cow've run dry, and th' owd hins 'ont lay.
And I aint had a mite o' food ter day.
I'll hev some pork ter night; I killed me sow;
That bile in that there pot; thass riddy now.

Yar rabbit (I thank yow kindly), save a Sunday jint,
Time I've bin down ter Fox and hid a pint.
That sasspan bile, What? Can't yow find the lid?
That stands inside the washus, dew that did.
I pay that gal and she don't dew n' work;
Gret lazy mawther, traipsin' in the dark.
She say she bin bardsnazen in the midder,
I'll send her gooin' and hev the postman's widder.
Them mucky goats hev ate my tarnip crop.
What, gooin' ariddy bor? Why can't yow stop?
Yow allus cheer me up, yow'd better stay;
My barthday tew! I'm eighty-fower ter day."

WALBERSWICK - An affectionate ditty by S. J. Richards to Walberswick, once a medieval port but now little more that a small coastal hamlet :

"When God made this land of ours
And to the east coast came,
He said: I've bits and pieces left:
To waste them is a shame.

A patch of sky and heaps of sand,
A river and some trees,
A bit of heather, lots of sun,
Some wavelets and some breeze.

Some soft green turf, some singing birds,
Some marshes and some gorse -
What can I make with all these things?
Why, Walberswick, of course!"

A CORNER OF FRITTON LAKE - by E. G. K. H.

"I remember long ago,
  In the meadow there below,
Like a patch of driven snow,
  Fairy snowdrops used to grow.
Near the water still and deep,
  Where the lilies lie asleep,
Where the dabchicks dive and peep,
  I remember long ago,
Fairy snowdrops used to grow.

Spring is on her way again,
  Myriad voices in her train,
Find an echo there below
  Where the snowdrops used to grow;
They are grey and cold and dead,
  Waiting till the year be sped.
But the daffodils are here,
  And their golden buds appear
Near the water still and deep,
  Where the lilies wake from sleep,
And the dabchicks dive and peep."

SHINGLE STREET - *J. W. Gosling on a sparsely populated hamlet beside a desolate stretch of shingle beach near Bawdsey :*

"There's a waste of shingle where the purple pea
Lights the July dusk beside the summer sea,
And the restless shore birds go complaining overhead
With disembodied voices, like the spirits of the dead.
There's a tiny village, hard by Hollesley bay,
Where the changing tides war the livelong day;
And when the heart is weary here is safe retreat,
Beside the friendly ocean in little Shingle Street."

WOLSEY'S GATEWAY - *Mollie Tatum's poem on Ipswich-born Cardinal Wolsey, Chancellor to Henry VIII and one of the most powerful figures in Tudor England. At his downfall he was in the process of building a college in Ipswich to rival Oxford and Cambridge. The dream died with him :*

"Down in a street, away from all the glow
Of modern city life, a gateway stands
Of plain red brick. Not beautiful, yet oft
A weary traveller from other parts
Has gazed in meditation at the sight
Of one small relic of a great man's love.
No verdant green encloses it around,
No monument, reminder to the name
Of that same Wolsey, who when he was lord
Of England, held the will of all in sway,
And who, once dead, passed almost nameless
Into a foreign vault. Men of today,
Yea, and men of the future, can ye pass
This edifice erected in the height
Of Wolsey's glory, without one mere thought
Of its creator and his direful end
So full of misery? Could we not now
In this more tolerant age, weave in the good
Acts of his mighty life with those misdeeds
Which brand him tyrant, egoist and flatterer?
Would it not be as true to speak of him
As faithful servant to a slothful King,
An upright man, who for his conscience's sake
Fell from his high estate to that of a traitor?

Then if we thus revere his noble name
Let us continue in that work which he
Began. Let that same gateway be a link
Coupling his mind with ours. Foundation stone
Of a new seat of learning we may hope
To build 'ere long and thus perpetuate
His life's desire in this his native town."

Wolsey's fall receives a mention in Shakespeare by one defending him in a speech to Catherine :

"He was most princely; ever witness for him
Those twin towers of learning that he raised in You,
Ipswich and Oxford! one of which fell with him,
Unwilling to outlive the good that he did."

IKEN - By Alastair Davis. The isolated church on a promontary of the river Ore is the likely site of the Saxon monastery of St Botolph, one of those who brought Christianity to East Anglia :

"A rippling of great waters far and near:
From Slaughden quay to Saxon Snape's old bridge
The River Ore her loveliest reach flings here
Midst rich green meadows mounting Iken-ridge.
Here mingles with the richness of the breeze
The splash of wildfowl lured to the Decoy,
Here nestles Botolph's church amid the trees
In haunts of beauty that can never cloy.

Far distant now the time when swampy marsh
And white dank mists o'erhung this smiling place,
When demons rose with voices wild and harsh
To challenge Botolph with his shining face
Of purity and love: 'Go, get thee gone,
And leave us to our ancient spells.' they cry.
'For ne'er has mortal man set foot upon
This desolate spot alive, go thou, or die.'

But saintly Botolph vanquished them and lived
To build his holy minster on the hill,

And day by day his blessed Lord received
Gathering strength to overcome all ill.

When he, on his journeyings, the Faith proclaimed
To heathen people, with his monkish band,
Thus, tho' his minster perished, still he's famed
For holiness and love throughout our land.

Iken, so English now, embowered on green,
Looking across wide mud-flats, creeks and bays,
O'er billowing marsh, till Aldeburgh town is seen
Beside the blue North Sea, faint in the haze;
Dotted with tawny sails, out from the blue
Racing the shadow-clouds to Iken woods
Where 'neath the sun's warm radiance lovely and true
She dreams amid her hallowed solitudes."

TO THE DEBEN - *Bernard Barton (1784-1849) :*

"No stately villas, on thy side,
May be reflected in thy tide;
No lawn-like parks, outstretching round,
The willing loitereer's footsteps bound
By woods, that cast their leafy shade,
Or deer that start across the glade;
No ruin'd abbey, grey with years,
Upon thy marge its pile uprears;
Nor crumbling castle, valour's hold,
Recalls the feudal days of old.

Nor dost thou need that such should be,
To make thee, Deben, dear to me:
Thou hast thy own befitting charms,
Of quiet heath and fertile farms,
With here and there a copse to fling
Its welcome shade, where wild birds sing;
Thy meads, for flocks and herds to graze;
Thy quays and docks, where seamen raise
Their anchor, and unfurl their sail
To woo and win the favouring gale."

ORFORD MARSHES - *Alastair Davis:*

"Silence and sea and loneliness
And at my feet the springing sward
That greenly clothes the long, dim marsh,
And billows thro' endless distances
To meet the firmament of sky!

Silence and sea and loneliness!
No mountains here nor brooding hills
Dare lift their scornful heads above
The level long monotony
To rival this green magnitude;
But here and there small winding dykes -
That suck and gurgle in the flood -
Meander thro' the fenny tracts,
With banks of gleaming, wet, grey mud
Revealing at the ebb!
And near the purpling, seeded bents,
Grow stunted trees and whin-bushes
Off'ring a scanty sheltering,
Beneath the rainy wrath of heaven,
To the slow, strangling groups of sheep
And cattle browsing peaceably!

Silence and sky and loneliness;
For sky it is that claims me now,
Folding half England 'neath its sway,
Stretching immense from verge to verge.
There to the west vast clouded hills
Of wild, packed cumulus pile up
And, curling, crash in thunderous glooms
Adown terrific precipices
Glimmering "neath a rainbow's hues
Whilst lightning flickers thro' and thro'.
To eastwards smokes a dank sea-mist
And swirls towards me o'er the ground,
In grotesque, vap'rous shapes of cloud,
And lifting once, reveals a glimpse
Of ghostly landscape, then blots out,
With greyish sombreness, the view.

Far, far above, immaculate,
Hovers a lane of kingly blue
And all day long its guardianship
Holds steadfast 'gainst th' approaching storms
Like a great river flowing on
Between two continents of cloud!

Silence and sky and loneliness,
With curlews piping down the tide,
And o'er the greensward swooping low,
The swallows, and far off, motionless,
Some resting seagulls in conclave.
Then boundless space leaning from Heaven
Plucks all the littleness from man
And pressing downwards, whelms his soul
In solemn calms of Holy Love;
And carries him thro' the list'ning groves
Of Wisdom, Prowess and Ghostly strength,
And guidance gives of spiritual themes,
And grants him gleams of that higher life,
Indwelling, vast, inviolate,
That springs forth from the Lips of God.

Silence and sea and loneliness!
The daylight fades out in the west,
And softly o'er the glimmering marsh
Twilight slowly lingering down,
'Neath the dreaming seas of night
Hushes the murmurings of life!"

FRAMLINGHAM CASTLE - By James Bird. The castle, the largest in Suffolk, was home to the Howards and, in medieval times, the Bigots. In 1553 Mary was proclaimed queen while staying here, and it was from the castle she began her triumphant march to London to claim the English throne :

"Castle of ancient days! in times long gone
Thy lofty halls in royal splendour shone!
Thou stood'st a monument of strength sublime,
A giant laughing at the threats of time!
Strange scenes have passed within thy walls, and strange
Hast been thy fate through many a chance and change."

SUFFOLK'S LITTLE HILLS - *Muriel D. Brooke.*

"I stand upon the crown of one of Suffolk's little hills;
The quiet beauty of the scene my heart with pleasure thrills,
The undulating pasture land, the fresh ploughed field, the grove,
A thousand charms reveal to me - Poetic treasure trove.

Across the vale the larger hills of Essex dimly show,
The tower of Henny Church above, of Middleton below,
And on the river level, blurred by distance, greenish grey,
The willows and the rushes interline the waterway.

The winding thread of river traced, the ribbon road I scan -
See where unsightly poles express the artifice of man.
But far from traffic's artery, and distant from the town,
The little lanes go frolicking and whisking up and down.

And in between the river and the broad horizon, lie
The warrens, ponds and pits concealed from superficial eye;
It's like a patchwork counterpane, and hedges form the frills;
Oh! joy of gentle verdant slopes, of Suffolk's little hills!"

FEBRUARY IN SUFFOLK - *by Charles William Godson :*

"O'er the brown fields, snow-laden clouds
Their heavy shadows fling;
Hiding the land in mournful shrouds
While solemn dirges ring.

'Tis Nature's sleep; fogs, chilling damps,
Our very heart's blood freeze;
And gaunt and bare, like darken'd lamps,
Stand out the leafless trees.

And yet - like hope - in fitful gleams
The laggard sun comes forth,
Full loth to cast his chasten'd beams
Upon the dead, cold earth.

But lo! responsive to his rays,
The first flowers of the year -
Fair prophets of the sunnier days -
The snowdrops sweet appear!

We bid defiance to the storms
That welter through the skies;
And bless the gentle, winsome forms
That open to our eyes.

Hope conquers gloom, through all the years
It gently smooths our way;
And Nature, kinder than our fears,
Brightens the lengthening day!"

THE OLD BARN - *by Norman Keen :*

"That breaks my heart to see this barn today
Wi' thatch half gone an' rat-holes in the floor,
The ol' place lef' to rot an' fall away,
An' nettles growin' tall around the door.
I moind the toime when Squire of all these lands
Gave all his men a harvest supper here;
He ate his wittles 'long o' all us hands
An' drank his pint or two of home-brewed beer.
An' now it's all desarted and decayin'
With sparrers' nests and martins in the eaves
The splines and bits o' weatherboardin' layin'
Knee deep in muck, among the fallen leaves."

HAVERHILL CASTLE - *by John Webb 1810. This undetermined earthworks has now frustratingly been lost to historians and archaeologists beneath a school playing field :*

"Proceed my muse, and quit this fatal dale
To mount yon hill, and breathe a keener gale,
There once a castle rear'd its haughty brow,
And frowned defiance on the vale below:
But built by whom, by Saxons or by Danes,
By whom destroy'd, no record now remains.
Swept by thy powerful wing, imperious Time!
Aloft in air no ruin nods sublime -
No fractur'd pediment, nor shatter'd wall,
In sullen silence waits its destin'd fall:
No triflers here, of antiquarian breed,
On wild conjectures airy morsels feed:

O'er this lone site no virtuoso pores,
To add some rusty bauble to his stores.
Happy this fortress, in its proudest hour,
Could laugh a siege to scorn, like Macbeth's tower;
But now of former strength no trace is found,
Save an old weedy moat, and earthly mound."

A LADY'S TOUR - *From the 'Suffolk Garland' extracts from a delightful series of letters written hastily on the road and describing a very young Lady's Tour from Canterbury to Aldeburgh in the early years of the 19th century. As Allan Jobson notes in his 'Illustrated Portrait of Suffolk', she takes little observation of the countryside through which she passes, more intent it seems on good living and frivolity. The first was written in Sudbury on September 13th 1804:*

"My dear sister P. let me hope that your suavity
Will not take offence at my sport, or my gravity;
In describing my Travels I've much to relate,
And I'm sure you will kindly allow me to prate.
At length in good time we're to Sudbury come,
And (thanks to friend M -) have got a good room;
Good lamb, and good ducks, good pye, and good wine;
On which it is soon our intention to dine.
We've been strolling an hour, to survey this old town;
One street we walk'd up, another walk'd down;
The barges examin'd, and new navigation,
Not the first in the world, nor the first in the nation;
And are safely return'd, without any affright,
To our snug little inn; and shall stay here all night.
And now we are thinking of supper d'ye see,
So no more at present, my dear sister P."

The next letter was sent from Ipswich on September 14th:

"At the mansion arrived, how delighted was I
Such beautiful gardens and grounds to espy!
We examin'd the dairy, the orchard, the grapery.
And escap'd without injuring at all my fine drapery;
Rich cakes and ripe fruits form'd our morning regale;
Whilst new milk was thought pleasanter far than old ale;
And, when with reluctance we mounted the chaise,
I could not help singing out loud in its praise.

We brought away stores of provision and fruit,
And such as an epicure's palate might suit:
Two brace of young birds, and a fine sort of plum;
A sack-full of pears all as sound as a drum;
Cob-nuts, golden pippins, grapes, and mulberries galore,
Pearmains, red streaks, with nonp'reils, and many sorts more.
  Just before we pass'd over the Brett's purling rill,
We saw Kersey church on the slope of a hill;
Then to Hadleigh proceeded, which much we approv'd,
Secur'd some refreshment, and then onward mov'd
  At Hintlesham nothing appear'd that was frightful,
The country's delicious, the roads are delightful;
Such beautiful turnips sure never were seen,
(The roots are cream white, and the tops are dark green);
And I fear you will think me a mere London bumkin,
When I tell you how much I was pleas'd with a pumkin.
At Sproughton (you'll scarce think it worth the remarking)
The pigs were all grunting, the dogs were all barking;
Mr Collinson's grounds called the Chantry are pleasant,
An excellent haunt for hares, partridge and pheasant.
  And now to make short of this travelling story,
At Ipswich we're landed and I'm in my glory;
At a table well stor'd with ham, chicken, and pudding,
And a house that one scarcely can fail to be good in!"

Ipswich, September 15th:

  "Whilst at Ipswich abiding, you'll expect not much news;
I shall not talk of robbers, of snugs, or fine views.
The churches are numerous, the market place spacious;
The streets are well pav'd, and the shops are capacious.
  This morning to Woodbridge I went with a beau,
To smell at the mud whilst the water was low:
Yet the ride was quite cheerful, the country quite charming,
And the red coats*, tho' numerous are not much alarming."

**The dread of a Napoleonic invasion led to the temporary barracking of 7-8,000 men in Ipswich and outlying places. These 'Red Coats' manoeuvred and trained on Rushmere Heath between the town and Woodbridge.*

Aldeburgh, September 17th:

  "Permit me, dear sister, to greet you once more,
Not from shady retreats, but from Aldeburgh's rough shore.

Thro' Woodbridge and Wickham our post horses rattled,
Whilst the ride we enjoy'd, and incessantly prattled.
'Twas a custom in Suffolk, I've heard trav'llers tell,
To drink health to all friends who live round Wickham well;
But I'm sure sister Sarah was ready to jump,
When she found the old well was transform'd to a pump.
At last passing Snape church, on Snape common believe me,
To a number of sticks my attention directed.
Which for may-poles, she said, had been lately erected.
But this was mere joking, I very well knew,
For presently many tall ships pass'd in view;
And you cannot but guess how my heart was in motion,
When at length we obtain'd a full view of the ocean.
  And now at the Lion behold us again,
Where for two nights at least we've agreed to remain;
And shall great havock make with the Aldeburgh soles,
Which here in fine seasons they catch in large shoals;
And for lobsters, so plentiful here do they buy them,
I believe in my heart I shall venture to try them."

September 18th:

  "This morning to rambling was wholly applied;
On the beach we first walk'd till disturb'd by the tide;
Then we mounted the terrace, a beautiful place,
Whence the views are immense o'er the Ocean's wide space."

September 19th:

  "At length, my dear sister, your father's young daughter
Has fairly been plung'd head and heels in the water.
Having made up my mind that I'd have a good dip,
I went into a waggon that swims like a ship;
But of one point 'tis needless to have the least doubt,
As fast as I possibly could I crept out;
And, shaking my ears like a tragedy queen,
I could hardly imagine I'd really been in.
  But now the scene changes, and homeward we pace,
Recollecting the vestige of each charming place;
Till at Ipswich once more we're arriv'd full of glee,
And now for the present farewell to the sea!"

Ipswich, September 20th:

"Our next route, my dear sister's intended for Harwich,
So behold us at Ipswich remounting our carriage;
But, as travellers must frequently find to their cost,
There's a proverb call'd Reckoning more fast than your host.
  As Stoke Bridge is repairing, the road lies thro' the river,
Where, when the tide rises, the ford's not very clever;
And by prudent observers 'tis well understood,
That 'tis not very pleasant to *stick in the mud;*
So we tried the old bridge, and, as sure as a fiddle,
We flounder'd before we got half to the middle;
Yet, as money does all things, the workmen were willing
To prepare us a road, if we gave them a shilling.
This obstacle conquer'd, we drove on like Jehu,
Till Freston's old tower appear'd full in our view;
The Orwell's fring'd banks like enchantment look'd gay,
And gave a new zest to the charms of the day.
  Next to Shotley proceeding, we reached Shotley Ferry,
Where we find some good brandy to make our hearts merry;
But the worst of it is (tho' we laughed and are glad,)
Not a passage-boat here is, alas! to be had;
But we shall not be kept very long in Suspense,
For a small two-oared wherry is soon going hence.
  But now we're at Harwich and thankful am I,
Our inn's the Three Cups, and our dinner draws nigh.
But first for a walk to survey this old borough,
To peep at the church, and the church-yard go thorough.
On the opposite shore Landguard Fort boldly stands,
Well secur'd by Britannia's invincible bands.
Long, long may our Monarch the honour retain
Of being king of the Islands that govern the Main."

EAST SUFFOLK PANORAMA - *M. D. B. describes the Suffolk Heritage Coast :*

"On the eastern edge of England
  By the quiet Suffolk coastline,
Lies a stretch of sylvan country
  Worth patient exploration.
Marshland, woodland, bracken, heather,
  Grassy walks over breezy common,

'Midst the maze of gorse and bramble;
  Leafy lanes and busy highways,
Silent streams and tidal waters
  Alternate in pleasing sequence.

Sleepy villages and hamlets
  Picturesque, with old world flavour,
Nestle snug in fertile valleys.
  Or on gently rising hillsides
Self important little townships
  Rear their chimney stacks and steeples,
Rightly proud of urban features;
  Each purveying for their districts
Many needs for health, and pleasure
  Which in villages are lacking.

For the antiquarian rambler,
  There's a chain of noble churches,
Some of which are hereby mentioned;
  Corton, Covehithe, Pakefield, Southwold,
Walberswick and stately Blythburgh,
  Then there's Dunwich, vanished city,
Ancient glories gone forever
  'Neath the vast encroaching ocean,
But its name forever sacred,
  Still lives on in bygone annals.

White sea foam and refreshing breezes,
  Blowing from the wide grey ocean,
Yellow sands and rustling shingle
  Fretting, constantly in motion
Chastened by the eager wavelets.
  Marram grass, and rolling sandunes
Join the cliffs and shelving beaches;
  Panoramic stretch of marshland
Reaching far in misty distance,
  Native haunt of duck and heron.

Farther inland are the parklands,
  Noble trees in stately grandeur,
Ancient elms, gnarled oaks and cedars,
  Set in green embroidered spaces

All unmoved by storms of ages.
Suffolk punches, brooding cattle
Browse beneath their spreading branches;
  Pheasants stalking, slowly, proudly,
Brightly coloured plumage glowing,
  This their home, this peaceful pleasance.

Far from noise of bustling city,
  Far from fret of traffic's clamour,
Tranquil beauty in this country
  Soothing to the tired and jaded.
This the landscape where my heart is
  Loyal for ever to its beauties,
Homesick always in my journeys
  From its verdant woods and pastures;
Homesick ever for the furrows,
  For the earth that bore and bred me."

THE FALL OF AN OLD TREE - *in Playford churchyard:*

"Thou hast fallen: and in thy fall
A poet may deplore
The loss of one memorial
Which time cannot restore;
Thy leafless boughs, and barkless stem,
So long that green bank's diadem,
Now greet my eyes no more:
No longer canst thou to my heart
Thy silent chronicles impart.

Under thy shade, full of glee,
The village children play'd;
And hoary age has seen in thee
His own decline portray'd:
With human joy, griefs, hopes, and fears,
With humble smiles, and lonely tears,
Thy memory is array'd;
And for their sakes, though reft and riven,
This record of thy fall is given."

BY THE NORTH SEA - *Algernon Charles Swinburne was obviously in a melancholy mood when he penned this description of a remote stretch of Suffolk coast :*

"A land that is lonelier than ruin;
A sea that is stranger than death;
Far fields that a rose never blew in,
Wan waste where the winds lack breath;
Waste endless and boundless and flowerless
But of marsh-blossoms fruitless as free,
Where earth lies exhausted, as powerless
To strive with the sea."

SUFFOLK CHEESE - *With the cream of the milk taken for butter-making, Suffolk cheese was made with what remained. Known as Suffolk Bang its poor quality became the butt of many jokes. Poet Robert Bloomfield describes it thus :*

"It like the oaken shelf in which 'tis laid,
Defies the effort of the bending blade;
Or in the hog-trough lies with perfect spite,
Too big to swallow and too hard to bite."

ORFORD CASTLE - *Built by Henry II in 1165, its revolutionary eighteen-sided keep was never really put to the test in combat and remains remarkably complete today :*

"Beacon for barks that navigate the stream
Of Ore or Alde, or breast the ocean spray;
Landmark for inland travellers far away
O'er the heath and sheep-walk - as the morning beam
Or the declining sunset's mellower gleam
Lights up thy weather-beaten turrets grey;
Still dost thou bear thee bravely in decay,
As if thy bygone glory were no dream!
Yea, now with lingering grandeur thou look'st down
From thy once fortified, embattled hill,
As if thine ancient office to fulfil;
And thou thy keep be but the ruined crown
Of Orford's desolate and dwindling town,
Seem'st to assert thy sovereign honour still."

THE ORWELL - *Three tributes to Suffolk's major maritime artery :*

"Orwell, delightful stream, whose waters flow
Fring'd with luxuriant beauty to the main!
Amid thy woodlands taught, the Muse could fain,
On thee, her grateful eulogy bestow.
Smooth and majestic through thy current glide,
And bustling commerce plough thy liquid plain;
Tho' grac'd with loveliness thy verdant side,
While all around enchantment seems to reign."

I. T. Shewell

"Of Philip de Broke, of 'Chesepeake' fame;
Of Cav'dish who sailed round the world O.
Of Vernon who hatefully watered the rum,
(They nicknamed the felon 'Old Grog O')
But more than all these, I tell of a star
Which shines in the East like a jewel.
Sparkling enchantingly down to the sea
The wonder of Suffolk - The Orwell."

"Who can o'er thy summer tide
  Wandering Orwell, ever glide
But, with raptured eye, confess
  To many scenes of loveliness
Spreading far thy banks along
  Subjects meet for poet's song."

TOMB OF GUTHRUN THE DANE - *By Nathan Drake, MD. The Danish King Guthrun is thought to have resided and died in Hadleigh. A tomb in St Mary's Church is thought to mark the site of his grave, though this is purely conjectural:*

"O stay thee, stranger, o'er this hallow'd ground
In solemn silence pause! there sleeps the chief
Whom royal Alfred, with a Christian's zeal,
From deeds of savage slaughter, from the rites
Of Odin, bath'd in blood and breathing war,
Turn'd to the living God : - GUTHRUN THE DANE."

VILLAGE IDYLL - Rosalind Mayhew writing on Harkstead :

"There's a village here in England
Where the old world lingers still
Where the ways of men are quiet
And where life flows on at will.
There's a joy of spring-time brightness,
And a keenness in the air,
And a clear unsullied vision,
Which is seldom found elsewhere.

There are people there who love me
And would give me all they could
There are violets there in April
Which blossom in the wood.
They've a blacksmith's shop and forge there
Where the fiery sparks spring high.
And when my spirit passes
'Tis there that I would lie."

DAYS OF AUTUMN - Bernard Barton:

"The bolder charms of savage scenery may,
Auspiciously beheld, demand delight;
Enforcing admiration, and delay
Thy softer charms more willingly invite;
But though the former fill the roving sight
With mute astonishment; yet soon it grows
Sated with wonder, and, bewildered quite,
Longs for some scene on which it may repose,
Such scenes as thy sweet Banks so lavishly disclose.

Nor was the distant Scenery aught surpassed
By nearer objects; there, expanding wide,
And by unclouded sunshine brightly glassed,
Flow'd Orwell! thy serenely rippled tide;
Hemm'd in by hilly slopes on every side,
Whose tufted Woods upon its margin break;
It more resembled, as by us described,
Some quietly reposing Inland lake
Than ocean's briny branch, which ebb and flow o'ertake."

BUTLEY - *A pastoral song written at Butley in 1792 by the Rev. John Black. Fair Donegall refers to Barbara, wife of the Marquis of Donegall, who occasionally resided here:*

"Ye shepherds round Butley who stray,
Attending you sable-faced sheep,
Drive sorrow and care far away!
Give your tears, and your sighs to the deep!
See, how the old abbey looks gay!
No ivy now creeps o'er its wall;
Its columns of smoke curling play,
In honour of fair Donegall!"

GLEANING TIME IN SUFFOLK - *An old poem describes a harassed mother mustering her children for a gleaning expedition to the neighbouring fields following the harvest :*

"Why, listen yow - be quiet bo'! - the bell is tolling eight -
Why don't yow mind what yow're about? - We're allers kind o' late!
Now, Mary, get that mawther dressed - oh dear! how slow you fare -
There come a lot o' gleaners now. - Maw', don't stand gawkin' there!

Now, Janie, goo get that 'ere coach*, an' put them pillars in -
Oh! won't I give it yow, my dear, if I do once begin!
Get that 'ere bottle, too - ah, yow may well stand there an' sneer;
What will yowr father say, d'ye think, if we don't taak his beer?

Come, Willie! - Jane, where is he gone? Goo yow an' fetch that child
If yow don't move them legs of yow'rn, yow'll maak me kind o' riled!
There, lock the door, an' lay the key behind that 'ere old plate;
An' Jemmy, yow run on afore, and ope the wharefeld gate.

Well here we be at last - oh, dear! how fast my heart do beat!
Now, Jane, set yow by this 'ere coach, an' don't yow leave yowr seat
Till that 'ere precious child's asleep; then bring yow that 'ere sack
An' see if yow can't try today to kin' o' bend yowr back!
Yow'll all wish, when the winter come, and yow ha'en't got no bread,
That for all drawlin' about so, yow'd harder wrought instead:
For all yowr father 'arn most goo old Skin'em's rent to pay,
And Mister Last, the shoemarker; so work yow hard, I pray.

Dear me! there goo the bell agin - 'tis seven, I declare;
An' we don't 'pear to have got none; - the gleanin' now don't fare
To be worth nothin'; but I think - as far as I can tell -
We'll try a coomb, somehow, to scratch, if we be 'live an' well."

* *home-made pram or cart*

A SUMMER EVENING IN MID SUFFOLK

"The bees sing home from clover far away
Over fields and hedgerows one by one
Laden with honey at the close of day.
Clustering on the hive in the sinking sun,
Dancing insects sing around the trees
And touch the water like a fleeting shower,
The air is cool with a gentle breeze,
Bringing the fragrance of beans in flower,
Then falls the peace of a summer night,
The bats come out and flitter around
A star shines out in the fading light,
The dew is gathering upon the ground,
Cuckoo calls softly his evening song
Away in fields where skylarks rest . . "

THE LAMENTATION OF BECCLES - *Describing the last of the four disastrous fires of 1586, 1662, 1667 and 1669 which destroyed a large part of the medieval town :*

". . . With sobbing sighs and tickling teares
My state I doe lament,
Perceiving howe God's heavie wrath
Against my sinnes is bent.
Let all men viewe my woefull fall,
And rue my woefull case,
And learne herebye in speedye sort
Repentance to embrace.

For late in Suffolk I was seene
To be a statelye Towne,
Replenished with riches store,
And had in greate renowne:
Yea, planted on a pleasant soyle,
So faire as hart could wishe,
And had my Markets once a weeke
Well stored with fleshe and fishe . ."

RUSHBROOKE HALL - Awarded second prize in the Crabbe Memorial Poetry Competition for 1957 this poem by D. Murrell Simmons describes the abandoned and decaying Rushbrooke Hall. Regretfully his hopes for its restoration were in vain as it was to be destroyed by fire whilst being demolished in 1961:

"Nothing moves through this mansion now but light
that steals across uneven boards from right
to left, that climbs a wall and leaves a stain
of amber till the shadows in its train
prevail, unless the moon should rise again.

At midday, twinkling motes dance unperceived
high on the sun warmed currents that relieved
the fireless void of Winter and from there
drift down the stone flagged passages to where
dust films a casement, settles on a stair.

Peaceful in isolation and secure
for all its long neglect, it might endure
many a season still - Time would erase
with far more dignity than man this place
that bears its sentence with a noble grace.

Ageless it stands, unhaunted by the past,
and when a footstep breaks its quiet at last
no echoes will respond. Silence has kept
too long a tryst, the slanting rays have crept
too often through the rooms while memory slept."

ON A SUFFOLK CHURCH ENDANGERED BY THE SEA - C. C. :

"Inch by inch the narrow green,
The lovely sward that lies between
The village church and the hungry sea
Is stolen away relentlessly.

Soon, too soon the church will go.
Man's puny efforts seem to be
No match for that relentless foe
The smiling, shining, hungry sea!

Shall we live to see the day
When our church is swept away?
Or can man resolve to fight
So persistent a foe with all his might?"

ALDEBURGH - Poet George Crabbe (1754-1832) was born in decaying Aldeburgh, then in its last throes of being an important medieval fishery and port and before its revival as a fashionable resort :

"Between the roadway and the walls, offence
Invades all eyes and strikes on every sense:
There lie obscene at every open door
Heaps from the hearth and sweepings from the floor,
And day by day the mingled masses grow
As sinks are disembogued and kennels flow.
There hungry dogs from hungry children steal,
There pigs and chickens quarrel for a meal:
There dropsied infants wail without redress
And all is want and woe and wretchedness."

ALDEBURGH FROM THE TERRACE - Another poem describes the town during the same depression :

"Thy old Moot-Hall is but a relique hoar!
Thy time-worn church stands lonely on the hill!
And he who sojourns here when winds are shrill
In winter - peradventure might deplore
The poor old Borough - Borough now no more!
Yet, on a sunny day, 'tis pleasant still,
From this fair eminence to gaze at will
Over the town below, and winding shore."

SUFFOLK SKY - around Honington and Ixworth described by Robert Bloomfield:

"With saunt'ring step he climbs the distant stile,
  Whilst all around him wears a placid smile;
There views the white-robed clouds in clusters driven
  And all the glorious pageantry of heaven . . .
Far yet above these wafted clouds are seen
  (In a remoter sky still more serene).
Others detached in ranges through the air,
  Spotless as now and countless as they're fair;
Scattered immensely wide from east to west,
  The beauteous semblance of a flock at rest."

LORD BIGOD AND BUNGAY CASTLE - *The powerful Bigod family were a thorn in the side of several medieval monarchs. This traditional ballad tells the story of the consequences of a falling-out between Hugh Bigod and Henry II in 1174 :*

"The King has sent for Bigod bold,
In Essex whereat he lay,
But Lord Bigod laugh'd at his Poursuivant,
And stoutly this did say,
'Were I in my castle of Bungay,
Upon the river of Waveney,
I would ne care for the King of Cockney.'

When the baily had ridden to Bramfield Oak,
Sir Hugh was at Ilkshall bower;
When the baily had ridden to Halesworth Cross,
He was singing in Bungay tower -
'Now that I'm in my castle of Bungay,
Upon the river of Waveney,
I will ne care for the King of Cockney.'

"King Henry he marshal'd his merry men all,
And through Suffolk they march'd with speed;
And they march'd to Lord Bigod's castle wall,
And knocked at his gate, I rede;
'Sir Hugh of the Castle of Bungay,
Upon the river of Waveney,
Come doff your hat to the King of Cockney'

Sir Hugh Bigod so stout and brave,
When he heard the King thus say,
He trembled and shook like a May-mawther,
And wished himself away.
'Were I out of my Castle of Bungay,
And beyond the river of Waveney,
I would ne care for the King of Cockney.'

Sir Hugh took three score sacks of gold,
And flung them over the wall;
Says 'Go your way in the devil's name,
Yourself and your merry men all!
But leave me my Castle of Bungay,
Upon the river of Waveney,
And I'll pay my shot to the King of Cockney.' . . ."

THE COCKNEY CAT IN SUFFOLK - D. E. B.

"When Tim came down from London town
So debonair and fat,
The neighbours all came out to see
The scornful, Cockney Cat.

His blinking sea-green eyes surveyed
The liver and the lights,
And other toothsome cat d'oeuvres
For jaded appetites.

Disdain was in the haughty look,
Worn by his whiskered sires
Behind that mask inscrutable
Burned smould'ring jungle fires.

No feline blandishments availed;
He left his rural swains,
And wandered forth in field and copse,
And unfamiliar lanes.

No lesser vermin suited him,
His menu changed each day;
With wary crouch and cunning leap,
He pounced upon his prey.

A partridge plump, a mole, a shrew,
A fricassee of rat,
None came amiss, he caught them all,
The roving, Poacher Cat.

So all you feathered flock beware;
Furred ravagers depart.
To safer haunts be off at once,
Or you'll be a la Carte."

A TRIP DOWN THE ORWELL - with Bernard Barton :

"Sweet stream! on whose banks in my childhood residing,
Untutor'd by life in the lessons of care;
In the heart-cheering whispers of hope still confiding,
Futurity's prospects seem'd smiling and fair.

Dear river! how gaily the sun-beams are glancing
On the murmuring waves, as they roll to the main.
While my tempest-tost bark, on life's ocean advancing,
Despairs of e'er finding a harbour again.
Fair *Orwell!* those banks which thy billows are laving,
Full oft have I thoughtlessly saunter'd along;
Or beneath those tall trees, which the fresh breeze is waving,
Have listen'd with rapture to nature's wild song.

But say, can thy groves, though with harmony ringing,
Recall the emotions of youthful delight?
Or can thy gay banks, where the flowerets are springing,
Revive the impressions they once could excite?

Ah no! Those bright visions for ever are vanish'd,
Thy fair dominion, sweet Fancy, is o'er;
The soft soothing whispers of Hope too are banish'd,
The 'Song of the Syrens' enchants me no more.
Adieu, lovely Orwell! for ages still flowing!
On thy banks may the graces, and virtues combine:
Long, long may thy beauties, fresh raptures bestowing,
Diffuse the sweet pleasures they've yielded to mine.

When this head is reclined on its last clay-cold pillow,
My memory forgotten, my name passed away;
May a Minstrel, more bless'd, snatch my harp from the willow
And devote to thee, *Orwell!* a worthier lay."

A MARTYR'S MEMORIAL - *Rowland Taylor, a Protestant martyr, was burned at the stake on Aldham Common for heresy in 1555. Taylor, incumbent at Hadleigh, had been chaplain to Archbishop Cranmer, Chancellor of London and Archdeacon of Exeter, but was arrested within 6 days of Queen Mary's accession to the throne. The inscription on his memorial reads:.*

"Mark this rude stone where Taylor dauntless stood,
Where zeal infuriate drank the martyr's blood.
Hadleigh! That day how many a tearful eye
Saw thy loved Pastor dragged a victim by:
Still scattering gifts and blessings as he passed,
To the Blind Pair his farewell alms were cast.

His clinging flock e'en here around him prayed,
'As thou hast aided us be God thine aid'.
Nor threats nor bribe of mitred rank, nor stake
Nor blows, nor flames his heart or firmness shake.
Serene, his folded hands, his upward eyes,
Like Holy Stephen's seek the open skies;
There fixed a rapture, his prophetic sight
Views Truth dawn clear, on England's bigot night.
Triumpant Saint, he bowed and kissed the rod
And soared on seraph wing to meet his God."

CORONATION DAY 1821 - *Following the death of George III, the Regent came to the throne as George IV. A troubled reign began with his efforts to prevent his estranged wife, Caroline, returning to England to take up her position as Queen. Samuel Ashby's description of George's Coronation celebrations at Bungay on July 10th 1821 shows they were marred by Caroline's supporters* :

"At the King's Coronation all Bungay was gay,
And of loyalty's emblems made gallant display;
The sun rose in glory to hail the bright scene,
And his beams, thro' the day gilt the palm's ever-green;
The bells join'd their peals to the cannon's loud roar,
And the oak, or the laurel, deck'd every door.
Save that *one in a hundred*, where nothing was green
By a blank of drear darkness denoted the *Queen* -
Flags, garlands, cockades, mottos grac'd with the crown,
And shouts for the KING fill'd the streets of the town.
The common's wide plain, that to Bungay belongs,
Was crowded with beauty's and loyalty's throngs;
Where a bullock whole roasted - then barrels of beer,
With full two thousand loaves did the populace cheer;
Here a scene of vast splendour saluted the eye,
From the flower-spangled turf and the sun-beamy sky;
From the concourse of thousands in youth's festive pride,
Where beauty with manhood in loyalty vied: -
There groups of bold rivals contending for fame,
Hurl'd the discus, and play'd each olympian game:
Here stream'd o'er the awning the flag from its pole,
There the camping and cricket ball flew to its goal;
While the band's loyal strain, and the victor's glad cry,
With the chorus of "God save the King" rent the sky.

Thus proceeded with joy a proud day for the King;
But a sequel remains for the minstrel to sing: -
In the Town a few *radicals* lurking were seen -
Mrs Bergami's hectors - who call her a *Queen*!
Just at night these Saint Caroline Knights sallied out,
To put harmony, order, and peace to the rout: -
With a pole for a standard, placards, and clout flags.
Of faction the Fragments, the Scraps, and the Scrags,
Like a pack of mad hounds, boars, or asses run wild,
The Townsman, the Plowman, tag, rag, Boy and Child!
With two barrels of beer to get drunk - for the *Queen*!
To insult the King's friends, and to mar the bright scene;
This done, arm'd with clubs, and strong ale in their heads,
Like the Queen, crown'd with glory - they reel'd to their beds!

But 'tis hoped, since the Queen is no *fountain of honour*,
Nor can take the reward of her *bullies* upon her,
That the law will due honours, and titles bestow,
In the name of the King, from whom all honours flow,
On each *hero*, who thus his authority mocks,
With a PLACE under Government - found in the STOCKS."

SUFFOLK HORSES AT PLOUGH - *Adrian Bell (1901-1980). The Suffolk Punch, a famous breed of workhorse, proved the driving-force in rural farming life until the 1950s :*

"They tread so dainty where that burrow was
That let their feet in sudden deep, when we
First ploughed the pasture up, less green than moss:
And though there weren't no difference you could see
When we were drilling wheat, me and the boss,
They knew that place, and went right fretfully,
Like today they did at plough again, because
They still mind where that burrow used to be."

The plough lay sideways like a stranded ship,
With hedge-pole handle, cotton reel and spud
With which from share worn silver-bright, the mud
He pared; then straightened and again took grip,
Pouting the cinder of his home-made fag,
And gee'd and twisted them with the plough-cord's sag."

Extract from 'SUFFOLK' by Robert Hughman :

"But come, my county, let me build thy claim
Upon a base of more enduring fame,
That thou hast earn'd thyself by art and toil
First honours in the culture of the soil
That prime of occupations and the best,
Ordain'd divinely and divinely blest,
That peaceful life which Patriarchs employ'd,
Which Kings have lov'd and more than Kings enjoy'd.
Here, Suffolk, is thy theme for glory - here
For honourable pride and lawful sphere.
Then rest your fame, friends, on your faithful ploughs,
For here the staff of life abundant grows,
And blessed him that reaps and him that sows."

THE RIVER GIPPING - Anon :

"Meandering Gippin', loveliest stream,
That ever roll'd its limpid flood
Through many a rich sequestered mead,
And many an overhanging wood."

POLYOLBION - Michael Drayton on the Orwell estuary :

"For Stour, a daintie flood, that duly doth divide
Fair Suffolke from this shire, upon her other side,
By Clare first coming in, to Sudbury doth show,
The even course she keepes; when farre she doth not flow,
But Breton a bright nymph, fresh succour to her brings:
Yet is she not so proud of her superfluous springs,
But Orwell coming in from Ipswitch thinkes that shee,
Should stand for it with Stour, and lastly they agree,
That since the Britans hence their first discoveries made,
And that into the east they first were taught to trade.
Besides, of all the roads, and havens of the east,
This harbour where they meet, is reckoned for the best."

THE FIRST STEEPLECHASE ON RECORD - from Philip Orwell, East Anglian Magazine. A legend preserved for posterity in the four prints by Henry Alken describes a famous night-ride in December 1803 when, while a group of cavalry officers from the Ipswich Barracks were entertaining officers from another regiment, a Harry Hansum boasting the qualities of his grey, challenged them all to a four-mile cross-country ride "from here to Nacton Church." :

"On the breath of the blast
They are come - they are past -
Beating the ground
With a dead, dull sound,
As they speed in their midnight errand so fast;
The steam of their steeds,
Like a mist in the meads,
Veiled the moon in a curtain of cloud;
And the stars so bright
Shuddered in light,
As the unhallowed troop, in their shadowy shroud,
Galloping, whooping, and yelling aloud,
Fast and unfailing, and furious in flight,
Rattled on like the hailstorm, and vanished in night."

BLACK SHUCK - The image of the black dog known in legend as Black Shuck forms Bungay's town sign. In a variety of hellish images it is famed throughout East Anglia but has special significance here where on Sunday 4th August 1577 it appeared in the parish church during a terrible storm -

"All down the church in midst of fire
The hellish monster flew;
And passing onwards to the choir
He many people slew."

Phyllis Noble provides this haunting poem to the apparition :

"Along the high coast road that dips
By wood and holt and heath,
By breckland bleak and fenland creek,
Runs the Black Dog of Death.

And in those haunted ways at night
One scarcely dare look round,

Lest, dark and grim, thro' shadows dim,
Follows Black Shuck, the Hound.

He follows wayfarers, and he,
Who, looking back, should spy,
Silent and black, upon his track,
The Dog of Death, will die.

An evil whisper in the night
He leaps the churchyard bound,
A shadowy wraith, foretelling death,
Follows Black Shuck, the Hound.

Down the long centuries he runs,
Haunting heath, holt and fen -
For, as of yore, the Hound of Thor
May still be seen by men.

All through the silence of the night
He runs without a sound,
Light as the wind - slinking behind,
Follows Black Shuck, the Hound."

IN THE BUS - *One-way conversation conducted between two ladies on a local bus ride in Ipswich in typical local dialect by Kay Turner :*

"Come yew he'er Miss Blowers now, an' set along o' me,
And let me hev yer basket, dew, an' set it on me knee.
Hain't sin yew fer a long toime, t'hev a good ole jaw.
Cor yar basket's heavy. Bin gettin' in a store
O' grub? Well, Oi doont blame yer, mor, you're wholly doin' roight
T' buy yer new pertaters, if yer own a got the bloight.
What toime do this bus goo? I reckon it's toime that went.
Here come the conductor. Ain't he gettin' bent !
He ain't th' man he used t' be, afore he had that spill;
That shook him up a rummin, that smash down Bishop's Hill.
Oi felt that sorry for his woife and children, pore dear moites.
That seem she set up with him days, and his sister set ùp noights.
But then, yew never know yer luck - things happen in a tick.
Oi hoop Oi ain't a lingerer, cos I want to go off quick.

Yew know there ain't n' hoop fer counsin Alber's youngest sister?
Oi reckon when she pass away, Oi'll hev her aspidistra.
That'll look orlright a-standing on the corner on the landin' -
That oon't intrude on them upstairs. They take some understandin';
Bin there since the bombin' an' they doon't fare to want to shift,
And they're allus grumbling at me, cos there ain't a ruddy lift !
Oi see 'em eatin' ice-cream in Woolwo's, sixpence each,
But when you've six t' buy for, gal, they ain't within yer reach.
An' oices ain't that fillin' and the littluns eat a rummin.
'No more taters, Mum,' they say, 'Oi'll see what afters a -comin.'
An' talk about a-buyin' shews, an' kickin' out th' toes !
They hev 'em on fer half a day and the bloomin' cardboard shows.
Look, here's the driver gettin' in; Oi reckon we'll be off.
Cor, he's all poshed up t'day; he look a rare ole toff.
Oi reckon that's his army suit. Bin dyed but look orlroight.
They say that navy blew take best - that don't come out tew loight
He'er we goo. We shan't be long. Oi'll be glad when Oi git hoom.
Oi had the sweep this mornin'; he didn't half mess up me room.
Some of 'em are clean, but him, he fairly take th' cake;
You could shovel up a barrerful, from all the mess he make.
But still we're glad t' hev th' soot; that do the garden good.
And keep the snails and slugs away - well if that doon't that should.
Well, Oi'll be gettin' out now soon. Oi'm soorry I gotta go.
That's noice t' hev a little chat, the toime doon't goo s' slow.
Remember me t' yer mother. Oi reckon your still a bit shoi -
Yew ain't talked much a-comin, but you'll open up soon. Goodboi !"

A SUFFOLK VALENTINE - *Elizabeth Cobbold, mother of Richard Cobbold of Margaret Catchpole fame and herself very much involved in Margaret's story, was a poet and had a selection of her work published in Ipswich in 1825. In 1790, at the age of 26, she married William Clarke, a Portman and Comptroller of the Customs of Ipswich who was apparently about sixty at the time and in delicate health. His young wife wrote him the following lines on St Valentine's Day soon after their marriage :*

"Eliza to William this Valentine sends,
While ev'ry good wish on the present attends;
And freely she writes, undisturb'd by a fear,
Tho' prudes may look scornful, and libertines sneer.
Tho' tatlers and tale-bearers smiling may say,

"Your Geniuses always are out of the way."
Sure none but herself would such levities mix,
With the seriousness suited to grave twenty-six.
A Wife send a Valentine ! Lord, what a whim !
And then of all people to send it to him !
Make love to her husband ! my stars, how romantic !
The Girl must be certainly foolish or frantic;
But I always have thought so, else what could engage
Her to marry a man who is twice her own age ?
While the tabbies are thus on my motives enlarging,
My sentiments William may read in the margin.

On the wings of old Time have three months past away
Since I promis'd "to honour, to love, and obey,"
And surely my William's own heart will allow
That my conduct has ne'er disagreed with my vow.
Would health spread her wings round my husband and lord,
To his cheeks could the smiles of delight be restor'd;
The blessing with gratitude I should receive,
As the greatest that Mercy benignant could give;
And heedless of all that conjecture may say,
With praise would remember St. Valentine's Day."

THE DEBEN

"Thou hast roamed by Deben's side,
  Seen the ebb and flow
Of its radiant, rippling tide
  Daily come and go.

Thou hast down the balmy air,
  Breathed the influence
Of the breezes wandering there,
  Gathering health from thence.

Thou hast sojourn'd too awhile
  With kind hearts around;
In their frank and cordial smile
  Friendly welcome found."

NEW YEAR'S DAY -During a time of war by D. E. B.

"Here on the bough the robin sings.
The peace of immemorial things
Haunts the dark wood, the field, the stream
Whose swirling waters palely gleam.
The frozen fallows sombre lie
Beneath the still translucent sky.
And barren stubbles fringed with snow
Fade in the saffron sunset glow.
The lovely earth that warms my sight
Heeds not man's mad insensate flight
From reason's sway and mocks again
A shattered world still racked with pain.
Fresh from time's womb, the new born year
Quickens who knows what boding fear,
What frenzied, catastrophic hour
Winged with destruction's deadly power.
Still the impoverished earth each morn
Waits leaf and bud and flowering thorn.
Nor shall these meadows cease to be
Green with fair earth's felicity."

LINES TO SIR ALFRED MUNNINGS - on reading 'The Finish' by D. E. B..

"Whoi, bor, yow een't a' gooin' ter give up yit?
Oi rid them books o' yourn an' Oi could sit
An' read 'em threw agin. So don't yow stop,
But start on Volume Fow-er, neck and crop.
Oi wholly larfed when Oi had rid them letters
By fowks wot think they know more'an their betters,
The duzzy fules carn't even howd a brush,
An' daub th'owd canvas wi' a lot o' mush.
A marster job yow done tew in yar day;
Them hosses fare ter look aloive Oi say.
Well yow can paint an' yow can wroite, yow can,
Oi'm rarely glad, Sir, yar a Suffolk man."

THE DUNWICH ROSE - Still found here and said to have been planted long ago round the last old priory of the sunken city :

"The Dunwich Rose with snow-white blossom,
Soft, pure and white as is the cygnet's bosom,
Decks the stern and sterile cliff, and throws
O'er its rough brow, new beauty where it grows."

THE TRIPLE PLEA - At least two inns in Suffolk are called 'The Triple Plea. The sign on one shows three figures standing over a corpse with the devil lurking in the background. The origin of the name is illustrated in this old verse :

"Law, Physic and Divinity,
Being in dispute could not agree
To settle which among them three
Should have the superiority.

Law pleads he does preserve men's lands
And all their goods from ravengers' hands;
Therefore of right he challenged he
Should have the superiority.

Physic prescribes receipts for health,
Which men prefer before their wealth;
Therefore of right he challenged he
Should have the superiority.

Then straight steps up the priest demure
Who of men's souls hath care and cure;
Therefore of right he challenged he
Should have the superiority.

If judges end this 'Triple Plea,'
The lawyer shall bear all the sway.
If umpires then their verdict give,
Physicians are best of all who live.
If bishops arbitrate the case,
The priest must have the highest place.

But if honest, sober, wise men judge,
Then all the three away must trudge;
But if men fools and knaves will be,
They'll be ass-ridden by all three.
Now if them three cannot agree,
The devil shall ride them three times three."

TO SUFFOLK - *And finally a poem by Cecil H. Lay which describes so beautifully how the majority who make their home here feel about this delightful county :*

"When mavises begin to build,
And lilac-twigs again are filled;
When buds had thickened in the glen,
And ducks in couples sought the fen;
When sticklebacks were rosy-gilled,
And blackthorn flimsy petals spilled;
When frogs were stirring in the mud,
And chestnuts sticky in the bud;
Said I, when night shall equal day,
From winter quarters I'll away.

When robins fed their spotted young,
And catkins from the hazel hung;
When warbler flouting, warbler sung,
And squirrels on the pine tree hung;
When days were bright and skies were blue,
And yokels 'gan again to woo;
When thrush and blackbird early woke,
And leaves had bronzed upon the oak;
Said I, now cheerless days are done,
My pilgrimage shall be begun.

When swallows hawked in golden air,
And flowers were blooming everywhere;
When shores were gay and bathers bright,
And glow-worms greenly shone at night;
When hay was mown and cuckoos flown,
And summer held her golden throne;
When cherries shone amidst the green,
And apples on the bough were seen;
Said I, the time has come to start!
This home and I will shortly part.
When martlets left the cobwebbed eaves,
And russet corn was bound in sheaves;
When sunflowers bent their aureoled heads,
And spiders spun their migrant threads;
When skies were poems ready writ,
And morning mists were infinite;
When berries dazed the insect throng,
And leaves fell through the robin song;

Said I, the season passeth by,
My luck upon the road I'll try.

When winds were wild, and roofs untiled,
And coloured leaves in corners piled;
When bat and doormouse went to sleep,
And bough and sky did frequent weep;
When nuts were plucked, and medlars sucked,
And pheasant shot, and furrows mucked;
When suns were dim and days were brief,
And winds re-howled their ancient grief;
Said I, the road now calleth me,
A pilgrim once again I'll be.

When pool and stream were frozen hard,
And cattle strayed within the yard;
When elms were red, and ash trees black,
And sparrows robbed the farmer's stack;
When tilth and farrow changed to stone,
And hoodies fought around the bone;
When hands were numb and minds depressed,
When snow the naked trees had dressed;
Said I, I will away from here
In this hard season of the year.

Yet here I stay, and years go by,
And Suffolk knows the reason why."

ACKNOWLEDGEMENTS

Contemporary East Anglian Poetry - S Fowler Wright
Some LiteraryAssociations of East Anglia - W. A. Dutt
Rivers of East Anglia - James Turner
The Suffolk Garland
The New Suffolk Garland
The East Anglian Magazine
Allan Jobson
E. L. Fowler
Algernon Charles Swinbourne
John Lydgate
G. A. Squires
Victor Allen
Ethel Wynne Candwell
Olando Whistlecraft
Michael Cave
Robert Bloomfield
Reginald T. Bellamy
A. E. Tomlinson
Elizabeth Cobbold
George Crabbe
J. W. Gosling
Rev F. R. Knightley, M. A.
James Pattinson
Alistair Davis
Alice Cochrane
John Barcroft
Mollie Tatum
Mrs E. B. Cowell
Edward Fitzgerald
Agnes Strickland
Henry Dell
Arthur C. C. Hervey
F. H. A. Engleheart
Sir Francis Newbolt
Adrian Bell
Jean Inglelow
Samuel Ashby
Mortimer Collins
James Bird
L. B. Cane
Miss S. Evance
S. J. Richards
Bernard Barton
Muriel D. Brooke
Charles William Godson
Norman Keen
John Webb
I. T. Shewell
Rosalind Mayhew
Rev John Black
D. Murrell Simmons
Thomson
Cloudesley Brereton
Nathan Drake M. D.
Robert Hughman
Michael Drayton
Philip Orwell
Kay Turner
Cecil H. Lay